It's Not Your Fault

Structured Psychology
is all about you: who you are
and why you think, feel,
and do the things you do.

Rogers Follansbee, PhD

AXES AVERY PUBLISHING

© 2025 Rogers Follansbee | All rights reserved.

StructuredPsychology.com

ISBN: 979-8-9905806-0-2

Editing & Design: Leah Donell

Editing: Abigail Gripman

Dedication

To my wife and children, who never
tried to derail my one-track mind,
change my questionable sense of humor,
or improve my selective hearing...
while I was writing this book.

Acknowledgments

I would like to extend a special thank you to the Universidad de Navarra, Pamplona, Spain, for its unrelenting support during the development of my dissertation; Dr. Agustin Riera Matute for his knowledgeable guidance; and logics professor James C. Colbert, PhD, for assuring that I stayed loyal to the logic I claim to so tightly follow.

Special recognition goes to Ms. Leah Donell for her extensive involvement in the writing of this book. There will be no plastic trophy for Ms. Donell, only one of solid silver and gold.

TABLE OF CONTENTS:

Since every action has a cause, so must human behavior.

Our Goal:

Provide a more
just understanding
of why we all
think, feel, and do
the things we do.

No Instructions Required

As an early adopter of *Structured Psychology*, I think you should know, I didn't get it—not at first. Not for a while. Not totally. And at the time I thought I had.

You might also be interested to know that I have no relevant credentials or widespread following. I don't generally find myself writing books. I'm the one behind the scenes helping someone else's book get made, a creative type who happens to love books. Plus I'd always thought psychology was interesting and had even read a few of those kinds of books, often looking for the correct combination of steps or rituals that would bring me to that ever-elusive "better me." Or trying to crack the code of human personality types.

If uncovering a "better you" is what you've come to this book for you may be disappointed. Same goes for personality types. And you're going to review some mundane logic. And those guidelines and that logic might feel incredibly simplistic at first.

I've come to think of *Structured Psychology* as a cheat sheet for skillfully navigating human relationships.

An uphill paradigm shift

The author of *Structured Psychology*, my accidental mentor Rogers Follansbee had, over the years, educated a number of people on his findings, but failed to find anyone who saw the sheer usefulness of this information he had patiently schooled me on over the course of months and years.

Then, my personal experiences started converging in a way that resulted in what Rogers calls "contradiction overload." And in a flash of comprehension, I finally understood why he had spent so many years trying to make others understand what he had. All this while I was helping him finally craft a message that may convey these truths in a way others would understand—even embrace—as I have.

As I hinted at before, I came into this project in a different role than the one for which I received such a warm affirmation in the *Acknowledgments*. And quite unexpectedly, my mind was completely upended by this theory called *Structured Psychology*. It felt like I had been freed from so much mental baggage and psychological suffering just by finally *understanding* what this idea was all about.

As I began distributing this book to some early readers, they presented me with many of the same questions I had early on. So if you're new to this theory, give it some time to truly sink in before relegating it to that pile of self-help books that didn't manage to fix anything!

A way to search for *my own* answers

Ever searched for answers to questions about life for which no human has ever been privy? Maybe a sage here, a prophet there—the stuff of philosophy and religion. The things only certain ones of us, for our own very good reasons, have tried to sort out. And myself, I've looked in a bunch of places and entertained many inspired ideas. But they all seemed to miss the mark. Some ideal or lofty platitude would ultimately rub me the wrong way and my interest would wane until I experienced it all again with the next philosophy or life strategy that burned brightly at first but dimmed quickly. How could anyone agree with *everything* involved?

That's where *Structured Psychology* gets it right...which wasn't immediately apparent to me. You see, I was hoping somebody out there would just tell me the TRUTH already so I could go about my life in the most skillful and inspired way possible.

Many truths about life's predictable, dynamic ways are spelled out quite clearly in these pages. But it will require you to take what you've learned and apply it to your own very specific life situation. And it'll probably take a bit of honest contemplation and earnest exploration if you're doing it right.

What you'll be gifted with in this book is a way of taking in the life happening around you and understanding how you might better achieve your goals while working towards more harmonious relationships. *It's Not Your Fault* explores the ups and downs of life with commonplace scenarios that help illustrate the language of *Structured Psychology*. It will be up to you to apply these concepts to your life. With any luck, you'll be able to see why certain areas of your life aren't going the way you'd like and what you might try to improve them.

Slow and steady,
Leah Donell

Life is governed by a clearly defined Structure, without which human behavior would not be possible.

A New Way of Thinking

Since the advent of psychologists like Pierre Janet, Sigmund Freud, and Carl Rogers, researchers have wrestled to explain human conduct. Typically, psychology's most renowned thinkers have been experts at describing how we behave and offered—with surprising insight—their best assumptions as to the fundamental causes of that behavior. Unfortunately, instead of using science to find the answers to their queries, it's been intuition, insight, and good old-fashioned guesswork that's sparked their conclusions. As a result, the actual causes of the human condition have, up to now, remained elusive, and our general conduct no less mysterious.

In the following analysis of human behavior, you will notice that I have intentionally left intuition to the side and instead, applied a method of research that is firmly anchored to the same method of inquiry that all scientific discoveries have been loyal to over the decades: *deductive logic*. You will, however, not be needing any special degrees, diplomas, or certificates with fancy seals on them to understand what I have to say. All that will be required is a little common sense, a sprinkle of patience, and an open mind.

What are we looking for?

I think that most of us would like to know how to improve our lives, reduce or eliminate conflict, feel more in control of our emotions, and have the wherewithal to shape our own destinies. But are such wishes reasonable? Self-help books that assure their readers that relief is just around the corner, motivational speakers, and general advice about how to successfully live our lives abound and yet, rarely lead to lasting success stories. Why? Because, in general, the self-help community forgets that each one of us is as similar to everyone else as we are different. As a result, one self-help system might secure relief for Doug in Des Moines but not work at all for Meredith in Miami. And what might leave Carlos overwhelmed with doubt, may finally bring Ling the happiness she'd always dreamed of.

A little back story

In the mid-1960s, while finishing my master's certificate in philosophy, I obtained a degree in clinical psychology at the University of Madrid. There I'd been exposed to all the classical approaches to understanding the human psyche. What I discovered, however, was that with very few exceptions, traditional, mainstream psychology had little to offer as a truly scientific discipline. Indeed, it was all over the place! If something didn't fit into one researcher's preset scope of investigation, they would just make something up. Most revelations were unusually clever and insightful, but still just the byproduct of intuition—not science.

In the meantime, when it was finally the moment for me to prepare a doctoral thesis in psychology, I picked a subject that had always intrigued me: Anna Freud's defense mechanism "projection." (We'll get into this in Chapter 3.) My plan was to do an in-depth study of this mechanism, expose its origin, then demonstrate its prevalence as part of the human condition in general. However, I soon discovered that all the mechanisms she had proposed as functioning in the human psyche weren't mechanisms at all, but rather the "grandchildren" of far more important psychological forces whose discovery depended entirely on a deductive method of analysis.

After receiving my doctorate in 1974, I set my sights on testing and retesting the theory that had, in the meantime, inadvertently emerged. In doing so, I made any number of adjustments as to how my discovery explained our day-to-day lives and psychological well-being in general. Now I feel ready to share my findings and expose this new way of understanding what it means to be psychologically alive. My hope is that by understanding the true causes of human behavior, not only will we all be better equipped to alleviate the psychological distress many of us feel, but definitively understand ourselves and others with far more accuracy.

For a deeper explanation of everything that I am about to discuss, you may consult the website below. In other words, while reading this book, if you find yourself interested in a specific detail concerning how the conclusions I reach are scientifically anchored, or any other pertinent issue, simply consult my website or contact me directly through my website:

StructuredPsychology.com

Enjoy the ride,
Rogers Follansbee, PhD

Life is structured by a tightly knit set of immutable imperatives that determine how we think, feel, and behave.

CHAPTER 1

The Structure That Guides Us

Human behavior can be a spectacle to behold. How many times have you found yourself in some public space being endlessly entertained by others just being who they are, exposing their oddities and conformities? Who needs social media when you have the real deal right there in front of you? Scenes playing out in a shopping center bustling with human activity, like two lovers in a spat, or that fellow who just tripped over himself, then checked his surroundings. Was anyone looking?

Most of the time, you'll see others behaving pretty much as expected but, every once in a while, you'll come across behavior that leaves you dumbfounded. Is she actually shopping in her wedding dress? Other times, it's your very own behavior that mystifies you. "Why did I just do that?" "Should I see a therapist?" "What's going on here?"

If you happen to be a person who's interested in who you are and why you do the things you do, you have come to the right place, especially if you've been dissatisfied with the explanations of human behavior that you've been exposed to thus far.

Here, I will be stripping away all the psychological rationalizations that we've all become so accustomed to, and instead of using educated speculation to discuss why we do the things we do, I'll be using the same guidelines from which all valid scientific research has traditionally taken its cues: deductive logic. My goal: Reveal the lockstep relationship that exists between deductive logic's rational processes and the behavior of all living things.

WARNING: The following discovery you may find unsettling, but as you will soon see, is no more out of step with reality than $2 + 2 = 4$.

About you!

If you're anything like the rest of us, then probably more than once you've felt deeply ashamed, out-of-control, angry, elated beyond words, or so proud of yourself that you thought you deserved a Nobel Prize! Then again, you've also probably found yourself under attack by a loved one, wrongly judged by those you thought were on your side, found with your hand in the cookie jar or, through your own negligence, in the wrong place at the wrong time. You may have also noticed how you constantly judge yourself—sometimes harshly—but then judge others more harshly still. You may even have made countless attempts to get your life back on track, only to find that after all your efforts, you keep going back to your old ways. "Why," you ask, "can't I just get it right? Why is it that I keep coming across like some clumsy buffoon when all I have are good intentions?" Then you see the title of this book and you ask yourself, "Maybe this will let me off the hook? After all, it says, 'It's not my fault!'" But is that really what this book is about?

Yes, it is! But let's not get ahead of ourselves. After all, we've been told time and time again that we should be accountable for our own actions. And yet, we've also been told that making mistakes is part and parcel of being human. No matter what, in no way will I be suggesting that anyone toss aside their moral compass. Quite to the contrary, my intention is to underline our need to hang on dearly to our values and ethical standards. That said, from time to time, we have all transgressed the laws of the land right along with our own and yet, deep down inside, felt as if we had no other choice.

In this book, my goal is to have you, the reader, simply understand how and why your thoughts, feelings, and actions go down the paths they do, or from where your conduct emerges and why. Why you react to certain events in one way when others don't. And from where feelings of anxiety, fear, apprehension, and abandonment truly originate. In short, this book is much more about **why** than **what**, much more explanatory than descriptive, and much more about what is real than what is just speculation. In other words, what you're about to read is about how and why you are structured the way you are. And yes, life has a structure, and just so you know, it's unrelenting!

As you will soon see, The Structure that guides us is put together in the same way we add numbers or know that nothing can exist and not exist at the same time.

In these pages, I will explain what The Structure is and how its imperatives influence the behavior of all living things. You will discover an entirely new way of understanding yourself, as well as those around you. And although this new approach to understanding the human condition may first catch you off guard, this new perspective of life's ins and outs will open doors to understanding the world around you that you never imagined were even there.

A good place to start

Perhaps the first thing you should know is that the psychological challenges you face every day are not punishments for any past bad behaviors nor retributions for what you think are your inadequacies. Once you understand that we all behave according to the same set of logical guidelines, you will see that you couldn't be living your life in any other way. And yet, just like the rest of us, you've probably fantasized from time to time about some other more appealing manner of living your life. Just know that by the time you finish this book, you will see just what an applause-worthy job you've been doing so far. The only thing that's been missing is your understanding of what really makes you tick.

The basics

We humans are an entertaining lot. We can get just as worked up over seemingly insignificant events as we can over the obviously traumatic. Some of us hide our feelings to avoid conflict, judge others, or are judged in error. We become emotionally affected by the reactions of friends and family for reasons that

Structured Psychology's validity can be demonstrated by using the same deductive norms that all scientific research relies on to reach its conclusions.

puzzle us; hate someone who, just moments before, we dearly loved; or suddenly become unrecognizable even to ourselves.

Since every reaction has cause, so must human behavior

Just so you're prepared, the theory I'm about to present, the theory of *Structured Psychology*, doesn't just focus on **how** our behavior is manifested but, perhaps more importantly, **why** it is manifested in the first place. Why, for example, some of life's events produce similar behaviors in one group or individual yet completely different ones in another. Why Sergio loves to play with worms while Gary is sickened by them. Why some people hate yogurt while others thrive on it. And why so many of us are perfectly willing to accept the norms of society while others spend their lives opposing them.

Researching the answers to these and other like questions, it becomes clear that there is an overarching psychological structure that guides these behaviors. It's a structure whose roots spring from our genetic characteristics as they intertwine with powerful but equally unique relational environmental influences. In fact, it is these two fundamental elements of life—nature and nurture—that play a starring role in everything we think, feel, and do.

Is this a new idea? Of course not! The notion that the outside world or environment influences human conduct dates all the way back to ancient Greece. What is new is the discovery of **how** and **why** these two elements of life affect our conduct to the extent that they do.

Information, not instruction

Now, I'd like to offer a whispered warning. This theory I'm about to present offers no magic solutions to life's challenges, no simple formulas to cure the mental distress life so often forces on us. This book will be very different from many others that claim they can save us from ourselves. Indeed, *Structured Psychology* has but one purpose only: reveal what really motivates us to behave the way we do. But stay alert. I think that you may be in for a surprise—it's not what most people think it is!

Relationships abound

To fully grasp this new approach to understanding the human condition, first know that there are several non-negotiable elements present in all living things without which life itself would be impossible. They apply to you, me, and the other almost eight billion people who presently occupy this planet. More importantly, these elements or structural influencers are not only directly responsible for *who we are* but equally responsible for *how we behave*.

The first structural element centers on the relational nature of our universe and, therefore, of life itself. In short, life is not a

We all behave according to the same logical guidelines.

stand-alone event, nor could it ever be. In fact, were we not relational beings, life couldn't take place at all. How do we know this? Deductive logic dictates it. Nothing can exist alone, so we can't either. It's as simple as that!

This means that all living things are either in constant relationship with their environment (along with its socially driven values, needs, rules, norms, demands, opinions, etc.), or life becomes immediately inoperable. What does this mean from a psychological perspective? It means that everything around us is far more vital to our psychological well-being than we ever previously thought, and yet our relational activity is hardly the only thing that molds us into the living, breathing beings we are. As a matter of fact, it's only half the story.

Psychological challenges are not punishments or retributions.

The second vital element that life depends on to continue points directly to who we are genetically. All living things, like human beings, come into existence ladened with a healthy collection of genetic baggage. There's no way to get around it. Whether we like it or not, genetics form an integral part of our psychological status.

As far as a living thing's genetic self is concerned, there is something quite unique about it. It's virtually immutable. For example, no one can become someone they are not. If you don't think so, just ask anyone who's ever tried to modify who they are and ask them how that worked out for them. As far as I know, it's never been done, at least not with any degree of success. That said, it's been proven again and again that we *can* change our minds, habits, reactions, perspectives, opinions, thoughts, responses, behaviors, and beliefs. Besides, once we understand what truly contributes to who we are and are constantly becoming, the desire for change, while sometimes intriguing, may not seem as pressing as it once did.

All in all, our true psychological point of departure is the result of a simultaneous blend of genetics and environment and their imperfect yet synergistic relationship with each other. *In fact,* each one of our individual genetic backgrounds is just as vital to who we are as is that big, bad world out there. ***It's the airtight relational union between nurture and nature that makes us who we are.***

I'll elaborate more on these points a little later. For now, I'd like you to forget everything you've already been told about yourself and how or why you do the things you do. Set aside most of what you learned when you took that semester of Psychopathology or Introduction to Human Behavior, disregard all you may have gleaned from any self-help books you've read, and give what I'm about to tell you your full attention. I can confidently bet dollars to donuts that you'll be surprised by what you're about to learn.

Just so you know...

You're about to enter a world you probably never knew existed. But there is a caveat to this little excursion you're about to take. *Structured Psychology* can only be understood if you're willing to think outside of the box, presuppose nothing, and simply read on.

Existence and, therefore,
life is a structured event.

All living things share
the same structural elements.

Influences from our environment
play a more decisive role in
our psychological well-being
then previously thought.

The way our lives are structured
determines both how and
why we behave the way we do.

We can't change
who we "are..."

But we **can** change
our minds, habits,
reactions, perspectives,
opinions, thoughts,
responses, behaviors,
and beliefs.

We "are" our
environment.

CHAPTER 2

At the Starting Line

Imagine that you're a giant bird that, in order to remain alive, must continually stay airborne, and in order to stay airborne, must continually follow the way flight is structured along with all its norms and laws of levitation. As long as you're on the wing, your life will continue as well it should. True, you'll have to deal with updrafts and turbulence, sunny days, and storms, but that's just life. Rain or shine, fly or die!

The above analogy represents who we are from a psychological perspective. It symbolizes the fact that in order to be a viable living thing, all of us must follow a set of pre-established norms (norms of flight, as it were), norms that, by and large, go unnoticed. Here, my goal is to reveal what these norms are in a down-to-earth, real way and how they motivate us to think, feel, and conduct our lives the way we do.

Are we all control freaks?

Yes, we are; only some of us are more freakish about controlling our lives than others. What is certain is that there is something quite rational about wanting to control the world around us. Trying to control our environment is how most of us get from one day to the next. Even those of us who are born with easy-breezy, go-with-the-flow attitudes will enthusiastically accept more control over our lives if we can get it. Feeling that everything is under control is, for many, a good feeling. Interestingly, being in control of ourselves and the world around us is one of

our primary survival tools, and with good reason. Life is hard, and the only assurance we have of successfully navigating its ups and downs is by doing our best to control the never-ending challenges it presents. Feeling that we're in control of our lives reassures us, affirming our ability to face life's abundant contradictions. And yes, as will come as no surprise to you, life is full to the brim with contradictions.

Where do these contradictions come from? They come from our environment, and there are endless numbers of them. Many contradictions appear as tiny or not so tiny tests or dares, like seeing if we can reach the end of the month debt-free, arrive on time to work every day, neither eat too much nor too little, be

> Life is full of contradictions
> that challenge the control
> we have over our environment
> and, therefore, over ourselves.
>
> Since contradictions are illogical
> and we are logical beings,
> we logically reject contradictions.

adventurous but not foolhardy, deal with a goal that has been denied us, or try to establish friendships that are supportive while fending off those that are not. The list goes on and on as we flap our wings, trying to stay above ground and do our best to learn more and more about who we are.

Life as a giant mirror

In a similar way that the human eye can't see itself unless its image is reflected back by an outside surface, the only place we can go to acquire knowledge of our selves is our environment. Indeed, it's our environment that has the daunting task of reflecting back to us its best guess as to *who* and *what* we are. Is there any other way we could know these things? No, there

We can be identified by our *needs* and *goals*.

isn't! Our environment's reflective nature is all we've got, so embrace it warmly; it's our primary source of life.

Everything and everybody that surrounds us provides us with endless amounts of relational information, and thanks to our five sensory pathways—sight, sound, touch, taste, and smell—we're able to know what that information is.

What's important to remember is that it's impossible to know who and what we are without our environment's reflective capabilities. It's our environment—and only our environment—that can inform us as to our successes and failures and our rights and wrongs. But it doesn't end there. As I just mentioned, it also is responsible for keeping us physically and mentally alive. No wonder what we *think* others think of us reigns supreme in our psyches as slowly but surely our "selves" begin to form and our identities emerge.

Speaking of identities, much like a coin that can't be what it is without both of its sides, we can't be viable living creatures with viable living selves until who we are genetically forms an inseparable bond with everything around us. If we didn't have an environment to relate to, we wouldn't have the faintest clue as to who we are, nor could we even exist at all. In essence, we are package deals; each one of us born from very specific genetic backgrounds that can't survive unless they relate to the world around them. What does this tell us about how we might be structured? It tells us that, among other things, *we are our environment*, and for the same structural reason, *our environment is us*.

Who did I say we were?

In reality, trying to describe, in any meaningful detail, who each one of us is could fill tomes. Nevertheless, for the sake of expediency, there is one tried-and-true way of loosely identifying who someone is. By simply identifying what a person's needs and goals are, you'll be well on your way to identifying who they are. As for us individuals, not everyone knows what their own *needs and goals* might be, much less anyone else's. But as life progresses, such personal indicators slowly but surely reveal themselves, allowing us to have a better-formed, yet perhaps still imperfect idea of who we might be.

About the environment and who we are genetically

Our lives depend entirely on the relationships our genetic selves establish with our environments and, equally so, the only way we can know how to identify who we are genetically. Only those things and people around us can applaud our successes or boo our failures, support us or leave us to the wolves. Equally so, it is exclusively thanks to our environment that we're able to know that we dislike spinach, enjoy music, are stimulated by the color blue, and are good at math, etc. In reality, without each one of our individual environmental sounding boards, we wouldn't even know our names.

From a psychological perspective, whatever relational interaction one may have with their environment, it will have an emotionally charged impact on them. The psychologically relevant events we experience may provide us with joy or sadness, a sense of well-being or anxiety, elation or despair. In essence, whatever the relationship we may have with our environment, it will always be psychologically meaningful to us. It must. It's a vital part of who we are; so vital, indeed, that our very lives depend on its messaging.

> ## Our environment is the primary source of our future development as human beings.

Our genetic lives and our environment

We are all born with a genetic past that then creates a genetic self with a series of genetically formed traits and tendencies. It's the genetic self that, in order to continue "being," will then relate to its environment, creating the persons we are. If and when someone or something denies or contradicts one of our needs or goals (the persons we are), we will logically oppose, deny, or contradict that contradiction. This, because we are rigorously logical beings, and if there's one thing logic doesn't get along with, it's contradiction.

If, for example, you don't like some thing or event, it will be because you sense that that thing or event is contradictory to one of your needs or goals. In other words, it has the potential of contradicting who you are and, as a result, deny the reality of who you are. When that happens, The Structure will demand that you act out your rejection of that contradiction. Why? Because you can leave no doubt, neither for yourself nor the logically driven world around you, that you are unwilling and unable to identify with something that is logically impossible.

Keep in mind that all logical contradictions are contradictions because they are impossible. For example, if you want or need a vacation, who you are at that moment is someone who wants or needs some time off. However, if you are told that a vacation is not possible, that fact will be in direct contradiction to who you are and, therefore, you will react accordingly (feel disappointed, frustrated, angry, and dissatisfied). As a result, you might grumble, complain to a friend, or argue with whoever it was that told you that you couldn't be YOU! You don't behave this way to annoy anyone, make a scene, or be a jerk; you're just following the reality of The Structure that obliges us all to disassociate ourselves from contradiction. Your behavior is not voluntary, we are all just structured that way.

When environmental circumstances are such that their rules and demands coincide with the rules and demands of one's genetic self, life usually moves happily along. However, when circumstances obstruct, resist, or deny who one is, a relational contradiction will appear and, along with that, contradiction.

In the strictest of terms, any circumstance that contradicts who you are (i.e., keeps you from fulfilling one or more of your needs or goals) will have an emotional impact on you and guide you to behave in contradiction to the contradiction you've received. This with the logical intention of neutralizing the offending event. However, any relational incident that supports or satisfies your needs and goals will create positive, confirming emotions. Come what may, rain or shine, as you soar about in smooth or turbulent air, *these two fundamental options of life—contradiction or affirmation—are what will motivate you to think, feel, and behave the way you do.*

We can only know ourselves through our environment's *questionable* interpretation of who and what we are.

Given that you are structured in exclusively logical ways, when contradiction rears its ugly head, you will naturally do your very best to resist that contradiction and, at the same time, make sure that you manifest your rejection of the contradiction itself. Let's say, for example, that you need to get to work by 8 a.m., but there's an accident on the freeway and you find yourself stuck in traffic. From a structural standpoint, the situation you're relating to directly contradicts who you are (you are someone who wants and needs to arrive at work at 8 a.m., but now you can't). Remember, your environment forms an intimate part of who you are and yet, at the moment, who you are environmentally contradicts who you are as a total self. How does this circumstance affect your conduct? It will frustrate and anger you. Your heart will beat faster, and you'll feel anxious. You

may bang your fist on the steering wheel and honk your horn in protest. No matter how you may display your resistance to this contradictory event (contradictory to your needs and goals) the reactions you have will be a direct reflection of the logical contradiction you are experiencing.

Take note that even though each of us will act a little differently when confronted with contradiction, contradiction's illogical nature is always felt in similar ways by all. We all shift into rejection mode.

Again, in sharp contrast with what happens when a relationship is contradictory, when the relationships you have coincide with the person you are (i.e., coincide with your needs and goals), only positive behaviors will follow. For example, pressed to arrive on time to the office, if you find that the freeway is almost empty, you might think pleasant thoughts, turn on the radio, and do a little singalong. In other words, structurally speaking, negative feedback from our environment will affect us negatively, while positive echo will do just the opposite. I hope that this not-so-astounding discovery doesn't come as a surprise to you. It shouldn't. It's only logical. If there is anything reasonably new

> There are two fundamental kinds of relational confirmation: *affirmation* and *contradiction*.

about this discovery, it's just how intensely your psychological status in life depends on life's logically structured ways.

Allow me another example of this kind of structured dynamic in action. Imagine that you're walking along a mountain trail and suddenly you feel thirsty. You need/want to drink some water. Structurally speaking, you're identified as a person who needs a drink of water, and yet you realize that there's no water to be found. In other words, part of you (your environmental self) is telling you that you can't be you! As a result, the pain you feel from dehydration will make you anxious and maybe even frightened. Now the walk you're on may become more of a chore than a pleasure, and awaken emotions inside you of negativity instead of positivity.

The vital nature of our environment's feedback

Structurally speaking, although we are relational beings, we still need to know when our relational lives are going our way and when they're not. How, for example, do we become aware that the air conditioner that's cooling us is on or off, the cologne we got for Christmas is too strong, if the steak we ordered is too rare, or if someone likes or dislikes us? This is done through our conscious or subconscious awareness of our environment. In other words, it is the relational echo or confirmation of the relational activity we are constantly involved in that informs us.

For example, if you open your eyes but see nothing, eat something but taste nothing, or listen to a musical composition but hear nothing, something essential will be missing from the environment you're trying to relate to and, therefore, something essential will be missing from the person you are. The importance that our awareness affords us cannot be overstated. All aware experiences not only reflect the vital nature of our relational activity, but outline the essential nature of what we're becoming aware of: affirmation or contradiction; life or death.

I must insist that The Structure needs for us to not only be relationally active, but to also have constant confirmation of that activity. In a word, we must be in constant sensory relationship with the world around us or perish.

More on relational feedback/confirmation

All relational activity requires some sort of relational feedback, echo, or confirmation from its object world. Each confirmation solidifies the reality of our existences. This doesn't mean that each and every relationship we engage in must be conscious. Most are not. What this does mean, however, is that no relationship can be established unless some sort of confirmation, at some level or another, has been received by the experiencing subject.

During those times when the relational experiences we have seem to go consciously unnoticed, we still register them. For

Our desire for control is rational.
This, because we are logical beings and control
is a logically generated tool of survival.

example, we might suddenly feel anxious, confused or delighted, or maybe pleased, disorientated, melancholy, or perplexed and yet have no idea what has motivated the emotions we feel. In cases like that, rest assured that whatever we're feeling has been sparked by some relevant relationship we just had or are having.

Talk therapy and The Structure

Relational confirmations can come from only one source: our environment. In fact, echoed affirmations and contradictions (positive and negative relational confirmations) coming from those people and things we relate to are responsible for the

Anything our environment communicates
to us concerning who we are can—and often
does—have an emotional impact on us.

lion's share of how we feel psychologically. Knowing this helps
explain why talk therapy, under certain circumstances has, over
the decades, been so effective. Talk therapy gives the therapist
an opportunity to become a crucial part of a patient's environment and, in this way, echo back to them supportive affirmations instead of the contradictions they're used to receiving.
When done effectively, counselors are able to re-tool a patient's
perspectives on the life they're leading, thereby allowing them
to take back a portion of the control over their lives that they

may have lost. Today, by understanding how we are psychologically structured, my hope is that this process will become even more effective.

Is self-preservation an instinct?

No, it's not! So why do living things seem to hang on to life as dearly as they do?

In order to answer that question, we must turn, once again, to how we're structured. All in all, our tendency to survive is more a question of logic than anything else. Realize that since it is impossible that something be and not be at the same time, once something is, the only options that thing has are either to continue being or confront a definitive contradiction and cease to exist entirely.

Consequentially, all living things logically avoid death simply because death contradicts life. This isn't an instinctual reality; it's a logical one.

What about suicide?

Understand that no one takes their own life with the intention of actually dying. Hollywood-style death wishes are just big-screen fantasies. Death is the gold standard of contradiction and, therefore, impossible for human beings to embrace. So, why do people kill themselves? They do so with one and only one intention: to rid themselves of the contradicting pain they are experiencing. Indeed, I can promise you that, given the choice, those who are considering suicide would instantly choose living again if what was causing them the distress they were feeling were eliminated. Life is structurally incompatible with death. Period!

All relationships require confirmation
from the objects they relate to.

Contradiction is incompatible with
our logically structured selves.

Our "selves" are logical because all things
existing are logically structured.

All things are logically structured because
nothing can exist in contradiction to itself.

Though our behaviors may differ, we all reject contradiction because contradiction denies the logical Structure that makes us who we are.

Existence and, therefore, life is a relational event.

CHAPTER 3

Where The Structure Came From and How Far it Goes

When I set out to write my doctoral thesis on Anna Freud's defense mechanism "projection,"* my initial efforts to find projection's true cause turned out to be grossly insufficient. More than two years of research brought me no closer to unveiling its causal secrets.

Frustrated by my repeated failed attempts to explain this common behavior, I was forced to go all the way back to ground zero and examine existence itself to see if it had any underlying characteristics that could help guide me to the answers I was looking for. Not surprisingly, it turned out that existence *does* have a series of clearly defined, significant characteristics that form an easy-to-identify set of structural imperatives.

As I slowly but surely was able to identify those imperatives, it became clear that Ms. Freud's so-called defense mechanisms could neither be mechanical nor defensive. Not only that, but while dissecting the whys and wherefores of those behaviors previously deemed "defensive," an all-inclusive theory sprang forth that not only explains defensive conduct, but much of human conduct in general.

---

* In her work *Ego and the Mechanisms of Defense* (1936), Anna Freud (Sigmund Freud's daughter) described 10 psychological mechanisms of defense that she speculated humans commonly use to protect their Egos from unpleasant or unacceptable thoughts or emotions. These mechanisms were supposedly triggered by a human's subconscious when it detected that an experience might be harmful to the psyche.

Life, as it turns out, is governed by a clearly defined Structure, without which no existing thing can "be." More revealing still is the fact that this Structure, by its own imperative nature, necessarily oversees everything we think, feel, and ultimately do. After all, if existence has a Structure and we exist then, quite logically, who we are as humans must be as beholden to that Structure as must be everything that *is* in existence.

Boiling it all down

The discovery of how existence and, therefore, life is structured can be summed up by one stand-alone paradigm: ***Existence is a relational event.*** In other words, things and people exist exclusively because they are relationally active, and it is this activity that guides how we think, feel, and behave, a fact that holds true whether a subject is conscious of the relational activity they are engaged in or not.

So, what's next?

Now, for the sake of clarity and to further explain The Structure that guides us, I will be presenting a series of micro-dramas

> **Our vitality as humans depends entirely on the relationships we establish.**
>
> **Without relational activity, life is impossible.**

or vignettes that illustrate the core concepts of our structural lives and the behaviors they create. These life-like scenarios have been designed to highlight a number of common behaviors that should be familiar to most. Once presented, I'll then explore each one of these scenarios from a structural perspective while, from time to time, introducing new definitions for words and terms you may already use as a part of your everyday vocabulary but whose significance may be different when discussing our structured lives. Soon, with a little practice, you'll begin to spot examples of The Structure in action and, little by little, a whole new way of understanding yourself and others.

Out of their element

The intensity of the sun was zapping Heather's enthusiasm. After their first night out in ages, coyote calls woke them both. The air was fresh and full of exotic scents. Then there was that giant saguaro cactus they parked next to—it was all so unusual. But that got her thinking. Had she made an error in judgment, especially considering that her companion was not exactly the outdoorsy type—not that she was any Daniel Boone herself. That was clear, especially now that they were miles away from their rental car. "That AC is going to feel amazing!" she predicted, trying to reassure her weary friend, Bridget, who was looking more and more apprehensive as the minutes ticked by. Bridget and Heather had been best friends since rooming together at NYU. Thinking back to their time as undergrads, they were inseparable. She never realized how neglected she'd felt growing up an only child to two workaholic socialites who were never around. And she knew that Bridget felt the same, having a single mom who worked two jobs just to keep the family afloat. Meeting Bridget changed everything and had helped her see how much fun life could actually be! Before they met, they were both loners without any real friends to speak of, living in the shadow of a world that didn't seem to know they were even alive. They came from vastly different backgrounds and experiences. Now it was time the former dorm mates had a reunion road trip, so they picked the Southwest, where neither had ever been. It had seemed like such a great idea—at least at the time it did.

"These are totally adorable!" Heather insisted as she crouched down to let a tarantula crawl up into her hand. Bridget was horrified. She'd sooner let a rat creep over her eyes than let a monster like that even get close! "How is it even possible that we're friends?!" she wondered aloud as she witnessed Heather petting it as though it were an adorable newborn puppy.

All animate and inanimate objects in your relational environment contribute to who you are constantly becoming.

"He's so fuzzy! Here, give it a try," Heather suggested as she stretched the arachnid toward her friend. Reluctantly, Bridget moved a finger toward one of its legs and gave it an anxious stroke. Bridget was surprised that the hairs were rather rough, even though they looked so soft. Heather could sense that the tarantula was, quite possibly, more stressed out than her friend, so she bent down to let it scamper away. As they watched it retreat, they felt the relief of a large, puffy cloud obscuring the sun, making the hot, dry air feel a bit more tolerable, and were assured to see a large bank of clouds floating to their rescue. In contented silence, they made their way back to the trailhead, both feeling unusually alive and humbled by the vastness of the desert around them.

Relationships and well-being

Heather and Bridget had a meaningful relationship, one that helped them thrive as human beings. They were fully engaged, not only with each other, but with those animate and inanimate objects that formed a part of their quasi-mutual environments.

Essentially speaking, even those relationships we establish with less-expressive, animate objects are vital to the creation and proper maintenance of our whole selves. Our relationship with the family dog, a can of soup we couldn't open for lunch, or a fly that kept landing on our mashed potatoes all form the content of our psyches—our "selves"—and the persons we are consistently becoming.

Again, every single relational event we participate in, right up to the unnoticeable microscopic particles we breathe in daily, that touch our skin, affect our hearing or sense of taste or smell, all form a necessary part of how we develop psychologically. It is our extensive genetic backgrounds in relationship with the

> **Since humans are the most expressive of all living beings, they provide us with the most psychologically impactful affirmations and contradictions.**

world around us that make us who we are. In a word, we are just as much a part of this universe as this universe is a part of us.

To exemplify the importance that relationships have on our behavior, think back to the last time you felt down or elated, confused or self-assured, awake and ready to confront another day or unmotivated and uninspired. I guarantee that you will find that those emotional states were due to one or more positive or negative relational confirmations you had received, whether you were conscious of having received them or not. Not surprisingly, such experiences may have initiated from your virtual environment (that which you only imagine) and/or from your real or physical environment. A painful stomachache or swollen knee, a soothing breeze or warm bath, a night without sleep or a surprise party in your honor can all provide psychologically affirming or contradicting relational confirmations and, therefore, inspire you to think, feel, and behave in specific ways.

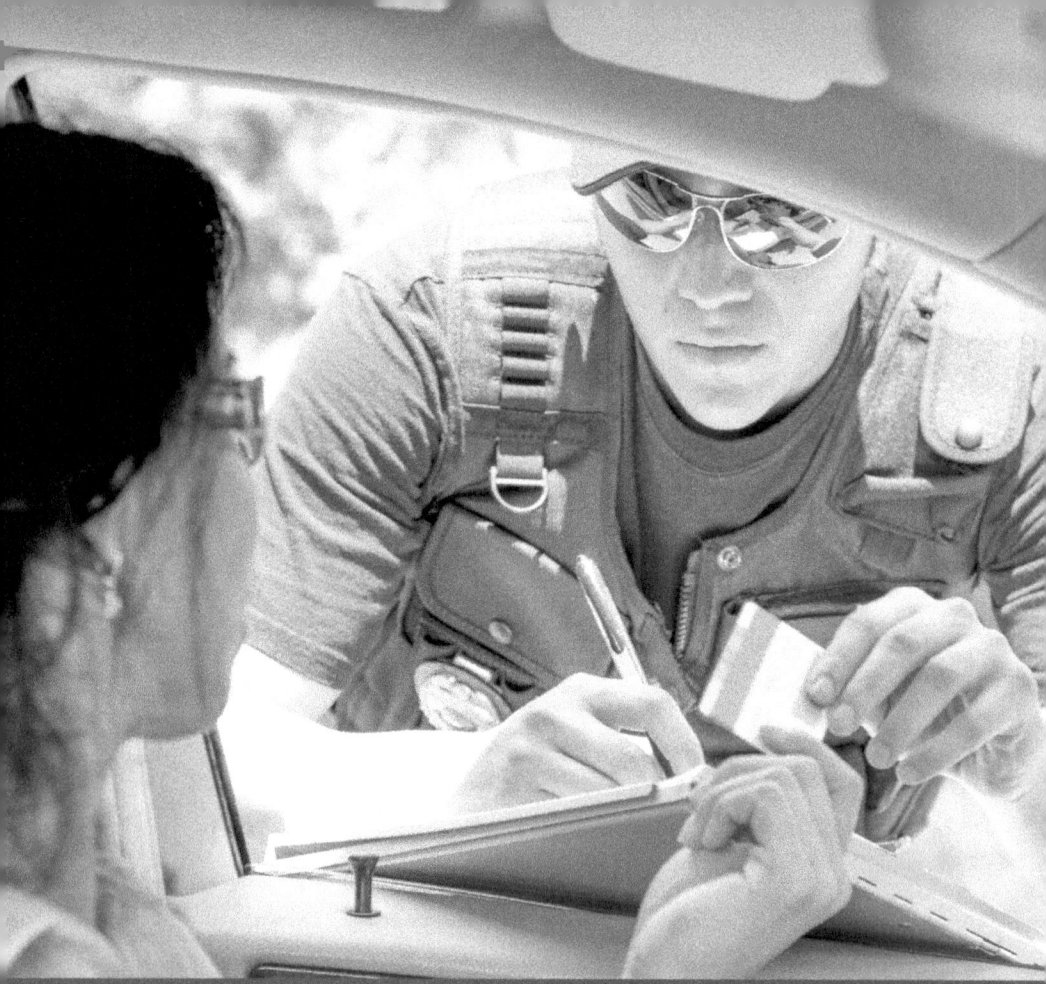

How we think, feel, and behave is a direct
result of the never-ending stream of
relational affirmations and contradictions
we receive from our environments.

The level of any relational object's
emotional importance will always
correlate with how that object affirms
or contradicts our genetic selves.

Relational confirmations (affirmations and contradictions) impact us psychologically, whether we are conscious of them or not.

Our vitality as humans
depends entirely
on the relationships
we establish.

CHAPTER 4

Our Relational Ways

As we've already established, there is only one way we can remain alive: by constantly interacting with our environment. This fact alone demonstrates just how vital the relational activity we have with our environment truly is.

What should we expect from the relational confirmations we receive from our environment? Believe it or not, most of the time we don't even know they're there. Why don't we notice them? Because they usually affirm who we are (i.e., meet our intentions, goals, needs, and wishes) and, therefore, instead of rocking our wings, they keep us solidly airborne. If we achieve our goals—whether conscious or subconscious—there won't be much to be concerned about. There will be no obligation to resist anything. We can allow ourselves to just go with the flow, mostly because the flow is going along with who we are.

For example, if we turn on the radio and hear what we want to hear, no further questions will be asked. When we speak, and what we say is well-accepted, we'll just move on from there. But if we put money in the bank and the bank loses 50 percent of what we deposited, that will contradict the goal we had in mind and, therefore, will prompt us to act out our discontent. Again, when the relationships we have are mirrored back to us in conjunction with our needs and goals, life moves along just fine. It's when they don't that problems arise, and they're usually of the psychological kind.

Life's key to understanding

Logic is reality's best friend, and vice versa. Perhaps it's reality's only friend. As previously stated, since we depend entirely on our logically driven relational activity in order to continue living, we logically will identify ourselves with our environment, and our environment with us. It's a structural must. Our very lives depend on it.

Simple, everyday contradictions (like a store that's closed when we need it to be open, or a phone call we're expecting but that never arrives) will motivate us to behave correspondingly and we'll act out the emotions such contradictions create in us.

The following is another example of how The Structure works in everyday life. Let's say that you are someone who wants to fly to Bermuda on a well-deserved vacation, but when you get to the airport you discover that your flight has been canceled. From a psychological perspective, you are a person who has just been contradicted by a negative environmental circumstance (your relational self needs to fly to Bermuda, but it can't). As a result, you're disappointed, angry, and poised to let your envi-

> **When contradicted,
> we are also then likely
> to contradict that which
> has contradicted us.**

ronment know that they really messed up this time! For example, you might complain to an airline staff member, make an angry phone call, or grumble to a fellow traveler. The world around you is not going your way (is not at all coinciding with who you are), and your conduct will reflect that fact. Life has ruffled your feathers and made it a challenge to fly right. As a result, you won't simply go along with the way your environment is treating you and leave it at that, at least until whoever or whatever is causing all this turbulence gets the message and stops being so disruptive!

A little more about that flight

Since we all identify with our respective environments, when yours canceled your flight, it blocked, denied, or contradicted who you were in terms of one or more of your needs or goals. Consequently, your behavior reflected that fact and, in order to maintain the logical sequence of your structured life, you tried to contradict your environment's contradiction.

In contrast, were your situation to have been the other way around, and the world around you had been in sync with your

Simply understanding what causes us to think, feel, and behave the way we do can help us to maintain our psychological equilibrium.

goals, you would have been happily boarding your flight, and your behavior would reflect the positively affirming status of your environment. You'd feel light-hearted, satisfied and content, helpful and understanding with others, just like your environment was being helpful and understanding with you.

The long and the short of this logical dynamic supports the notion that, as outlined before, we are *very much* our environment. Being that this is true, obviously, our selves are not created from within, but rather from without; a fact that demonstrates why we pay as much attention as we do to other things and other people. In the end, remaining a viable human being is the direct result of honest to goodness teamwork!

Your identity

You've heard it before, "You are what you eat." But this particular adage doesn't stop with a Big Mac and a box of fries. You are also every relationship you've ever had since you took your first breath. Interestingly, although you may be able to work off all those Big Macs you've been putting away over the months and years, no one can rid themselves of all the accumulated contradictions they've been involved in since birth. Those won't be going anywhere anytime soon, and maybe that's a good thing. They form an integral part of who you are and ultimately shape your identity.

Is that who I am, my needs and goals?

Yes, that's who you are, it's just sometimes difficult to identify what those needs and goals might be.

In reality, trying to list all the ways you can be defined would be exhausting. Structurally speaking, however, as we've seen, your identity doesn't come entirely from within, nor entirely from without. You are not only the subject of your life, but also the object of it, a fact that is embodied by the intimate relationship you have with the world around you. Your final you, therefore, is constituted by your genetic/environmental needs and goals, as they do their best to coincide with the needs and goals of your environment.

That's nice, but I still don't know who I am

If there is no well-defined contrast between what your apparent needs and goals are versus those of your environment, then it would follow that you may be confused about who *you* are.

Perhaps your environment has been so un-confirming, so negative towards you that you never dared to admit to yourself what your true needs and goals really are. Or, to the contrary, if there's been too much coincidence between your needs and goals and those of your environment, your identity may still be in limbo, leaving you unable to distinguish who's who. Just know that as time progresses and you increase the number of experiences you have, slowly but surely your true identity will emerge with outstanding clarity.

Relational confirmation guides behavior

In review, when the relational confirmations we receive from our environment affirm who we are, we're happy campers. We feel emotionally positive, and those feelings of positivity are then expressed in the way we conduct our lives. As we've already seen, positive relational confirmation (affirmation) most always produces contentment, satisfaction, happiness, and pleasure, emotions that often culminate in good deeds, helpful attitudes, and future-bound behaviors. But stay alert. That which might gratify James may not at all please Judy. One person's happiest moment may be another's most difficult to accept. This is because each one of our genetic realities can be completely different from someone else's and those differences can kindle any number of destructive behavioral reactions.

Bill, for example, may find happiness listening to Beethoven, while classical music may give his sister a headache. Nora may feel elated when on a volleyball court, but volleyball bores her brother Evan. Do such likes and dislikes, preferences or general aversions come from our environment? No, they don't. They

Affirmations inspire positive behavior, while contradictions produce the opposite.

What might positively affirm one person can easily contradict another.

come from our genetic heritage as it relates to those things and people around us.

When others positively confirm who we are, we behave positively. But again, remember that what might positively confirm me, may negatively confirm you.

For example: If Mike's genetic background feeds off conflict, divergence will bring a smile to his face. Whereas if Sara can only be happy when surrounded by peace and quiet, conflict will make her miserable. All in all, environmental confirmations, be they affirming or contradicting, are entirely responsible for how humanity in general feels, thinks, and behaves.

As we touched on earlier, the behavior our emotions create lead us to affirm life's affirmations, and contradict its contradictions. For example, if I affirm you by telling you that you're a nice person, you will tend to return the favor. But if I mirror back to you something that contradicts who you are—perhaps an insult, or a "no" when what you're looking for is a "yes"— the way you're structured will drive you to nullify, neutralize, or contradict my contradiction. This dynamic is to be expected as we are logically structured beings. Positive environmental echoes generate positive reactions, while contradictory ones just create more contradiction.

Now, let's have a look at how some of the relational dynamics we've been discussing play out in real life.

Caffeine boost

Megan was on her way to Café Presto, an independent coffee shop on Brewster Street. As she crossed through the third intersection, she was stoked to see her fantasy boyfriend Terrance in his usual window seat.

"Hey Megan," Stephanie, the barista, greeted her as she made her way through the door. "Americano as usual? And we have your favorite muffins in today." Recognition was a big deal for Megan. It is for all of us. As she placed her order, Megan watched as a statuesque woman walked in and slid an hourglass figure into Megan's favorite spot. "Damn," she thought to herself, "That's the primo spot for Terrance watching! That's where I'm supposed to sit!"

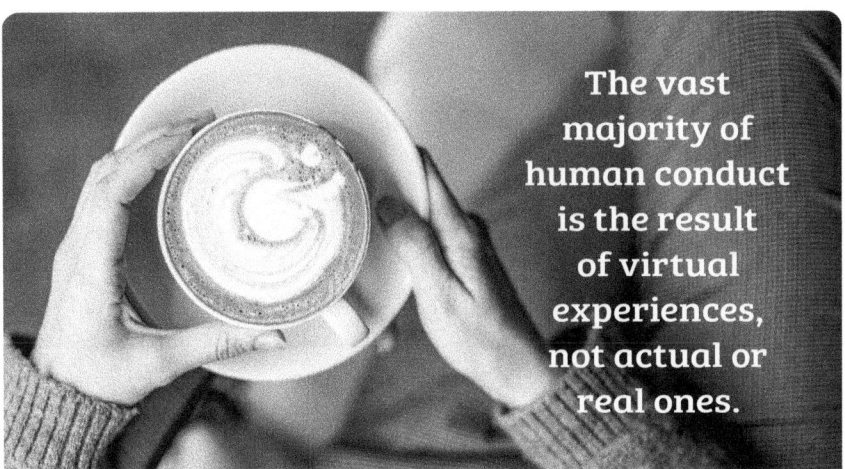

The vast majority of human conduct is the result of virtual experiences, not actual or real ones.

As Terrance turned to retrieve his order, Megan watched her new competition. She and Terrance were a perfect match from a sheer attractiveness standpoint. Terrance made his way to the woman's table beaming a thousand-watt smile and cast a witty intro into her pond. She took the bait, and Megan's heart sank with the ending of her virtual fantasy.

But then, just as she was deciding she'd better pack it in so she could retreat to the sanctity of her apartment, Eli walked through the door. They'd only been seeing each other for a few weeks, but she felt like he actually "got" her in a way that she was sure Terrance never could. Here, standing in front of her, was a man who she had an actual relationship with, and even in the beginning stages, had a ton of promise. And just like that, Megan's world was righted, once again, making her feel like she was desirable. As she stood to greet Eli with a hug she watched Terrance look in her direction and nod his approval.

Real, concrete affirmations deliver more impactful emotions than do virtual or imagined ones.

Concrete and virtual realities

Megan just took herself on an emotional roller coaster ride, most of which played out inside her own head. We all experience life both virtually (what we imagine is happening) and concretely (what we are convinced is real or truly taking place).

That's why Megan enjoys taking her work to her favorite coffee house. Just like the rest of us, she craves both virtual and concrete interaction with her environment. She needs social (environmental) feedback and will happily embrace a little fantasy while she's at it. Such relational interactions help us stay future-bound instead of just marking time. As we'll learn later on, it's our constant, future-oriented interactions with the world around us, be they virtual or concrete, positive or negative, that keep us psychologically viable. In short, as long as we're able to stay airborne, we'll at least remain loyal to The Structure's more vital requirement: never stop relating.

Back to Megan

While Megan enjoys her time being relational, she gets doses of both positive and negative confirmations from those around her. Sometimes, events in her relational environment go as she wants them to (they affirm her), but other times, seem to take a downward turn and go in the opposite direction. For example, when she arrives at the café and is greeted by Stephanie. This soothes Megan because she's being recognized, making her feel alive and valued. A friendly nod from a store employee, or a happy toot from a friend's car horn can be enriching relational experiences for our psyches. In Megan's case, even a simple gesture of recognition from someone she doesn't know provides a quick dose of positive confirmation. These are not virtual experiences, but concrete ones. Megan didn't imagine these things, she actually lived them, so the emotional impact she felt was real and, therefore, just that much more affirming. She had been seen and accepted. Even being offered her favorite muffin delivered emotional support.

Megan's relationship with her fantasy boyfriend, on the other hand, was completely virtual. It was just an amusing story she played out in her own imagination. The enjoyment she got from that fantasy, however, provided relational confirmation as well. Note how often, as life whizzes along and we find ourselves a little short on environmental feedback, we tend to fill in life's blanks by letting our virtually driven fantasies keep us relationally active in positive ways.

In our story, the reality of Megan's situation was a little less palatable, even contradictory to Megan's desires. As Megan watched how her own life-drama played out, it was clear that Terrance hadn't been fantasizing about her at all. In fact, she received one of those negative confirmations we've been talking about as she watched him chat up someone else; an event that happened for real, not just virtually. Since that part of her experience that day was concrete, actual, or real, it delivered a more significant emotional punch to Megan than the virtual story she'd made up in her own imagination. Clearly if Terrance had any interest in Megan at all he would have made a move—the man was anything but shy. Thankfully, Eli swooped in just in time to provide some much-needed affirmation to Megan's wounded psyche. And again, because his presence was the real deal, it added extra oomph to the experience that couldn't be matched by her virtual world.

More about virtual relationships

It's easy to understand Megan's fantasy life when we realize that our virtual world can sometimes be a surprisingly effective environmental surrogate for our relational needs. From an emotional standpoint, and in sharp contrast with the experiences we have with our in-your-face, concrete surroundings, most of the time virtual relationships are a lot less susceptible to contradiction than are real or concrete ones. Imagined relational confirmations, like dreaming about an up-and-coming vacation, or imagining what pleasure an evening's movie might

Virtual confirmations help us to remain relationally active when environmental confirmations are not available.

bring can, sometimes, afford almost as much positive relational confirmation as might the real thing! But not quite. Given the way we're structured, there is nothing quite as impactful as what we're convinced is reality. In addition, take note that the content of all virtual confirmations will be the non-verbal kind, and clearly only fantasies. Still, as I mentioned before, virtual confirmations can provide just enough relational zing for us to keep ourselves relationally active.

Actions speak louder than words

Now, for a little heads-up. Take care not to misconstrue the way certain relationships express themselves. When the way a specific object tries to get its message across to us is poorly defined,

confusing, or nebulous, we can leap to erroneous conclusions. Interestingly, we humans can be masterful non-verbal communicators, while at the same time, such kinds of communication can be easily misconstrued.

Certain body postures and gesturing can be almost as effective in getting a point across as can a spoken language. In 1967, Albert Mehrabian announced that human communication was 55 percent body language, 38 percent tone of voice, and only 7 percent actual words. Since then, others have suggested that non-verbal communication can take up anywhere from 70 percent to Mehrabian's 93 percent of one's communicative spectrum. Regardless of how one may parse the breakdown, the non-verbal way living things echo back their confirmations can have as much definite impact on resulting behavior as can verbal communication. At the same time, when an object's behavior is not clearly defined, we can err in our judgment of what that object is trying to communicate. One, therefore, should take care how they interpret the meaning of certain stimuli, especially when its interpretation is crucial. Asking for

> **Non-verbal communications can also provide positive or negative relational confirmation.**

a little clarification can do wonders to keep us at arm's length from contradiction.

Unconditional love, unconditional affirmation— more poetic than real?

Ever wonder if there is such a thing as unconditional love? Well, if we're talking about how we often relate to some animals, then maybe there is. Some pets can give their owners what those owners are convinced is rock-solid, eternal adoration. But when it comes to the human animal, love has limits, norms, and conditions. Enduring love requires endearing, positive confirmations, so naturally some contradictions, especially the non-reconcilable kind, can stop love in its tracks, and keep it snuffed out forever.

As far as our desire to have someone or something love us unconditionally, our pet dog Spot will probably come about as close to fulfilling that need as anything can. Sometimes we might have to cheat a little by hiding a sweet-smelling treat in our hand or promising a walk in the park, but many of us will still take an animal's positive behavior toward us as a sure sign of eternal devotion, admiration, and even love. We can count on our pet's boundless, enthusiastic, positive confirmations when, after a day's absence, they see us once again.

To the contrary, counting on our partner's unrestricted, enthusiastic affirmation when arriving home after only a few hours apart, might be asking a little too much. Many of us feel lucky just to get a curt "hello" when we see our life partner, best friend, or family member after a short absence. So why do human confirmations still rank higher than confirmations from Spot the dog, Whiskers the cat, or Fatso the pig? Because, as mentioned before, human confirmations are, by far, the most expressive of all relational interaction, providing the biggest bang for our relational buck!

Now, let's head to the courts to further explore how the relational echo, feedback, or confirmation we so vitally need from our environment can go terribly wrong, and force our self-esteem to do a 180.

Air ball

Rodney was off to play b-ball near his new school. This would be his chance to prove his worth to his new teammates. On his way there he replayed all the glory-filled moments as shooting guard for the state champion Bears. He'd taken his former high school team all the way to states, where he'd scored the winning 3-pointer in the finals and couldn't feel prouder.

Now he was in the middle of a radical shift in environment and even though he didn't know it yet, his life

We "are" our goals and needs.

was about to change as well. As he made his way to the courts his thoughts raced. There were a couple months until tryouts, so he'd play as much as he could and show his new environment what this kid from the country could do.

"Can I run with you guys?" Rodney asked when he got to the court. Everyone turned to see their leader's response. "Yeah, we need one more, so you're in! We're playing straight up to 15. Let's see what you got, farmer boy..." The reply was already a gut punch to Rodney's ego. Back where he was from, he was in the upper echelons of cool. But here he was an outsider, wearing the wrong clothes, and feeling out of place.

But then again, these guys didn't realize what he could do—at least not yet they didn't.

"Kid, you got point guard." These guys were fast and smooth, their maneuvers polished way beyond Rodney's farm-league familiars. And they didn't make mistakes! Up and down the court, the play never stopped. And since there were no refs, fouls weren't called.

Taking elbows left and right, Rodney had to keep his cool and roll with the punches. Nobody likes a whiner, but damned if those hits didn't hurt—both physically and emotionally. This bunch of players were rough and tough, and Rodney wasn't so sure about his skills anymore. He was getting pushed this way and that, and now felt too upset to defend himself. So he grabbed the opportunity, exited the blacktop, and head hung low, began his return home knowing he'd failed.

There would be no coming back from this egregious misstep. But it was painfully obvious that this was no place he could compete anyway. As he walked home, he felt as if he'd left his body, mourning his days in the spotlight as an actual contender.

Defeat, losing control, contradiction overload

That morning Rodney had a very clear goal laid out for himself—prove to everyone, especially himself, that he was a real basketball star after all, and earn the respect of the local players (be positively confirmed by them). This was the outcome his psyche needed as he headed to the courts, and it's what he believed would logically happen. Based on his record, it was a given. He was, after all, a real superstar. He just had to show these new guys that he was capable and worthy of a spot in the pickup game, and ultimately on the high school team. But that didn't happen. The goals he had set for himself were met with an endless string of contradictions, highlighting that the positive reflection provided by his old environment, the one that confirmed his athletic prowess, had little to do with the relational echo he was receiving from this new world he'd been arbitrarily plopped in the middle of.

Rodney saw himself in the right clothes, but it seemed that this new environment saw him in the wrong ones. He had always thought of himself as tall, but that met with another contradiction as he realized that he was short by comparison. As the game progressed his self-image got slammed with one contradiction after the other, shooting holes in his self-confidence. The emotional pain got worse as the other players treated him like an outsider, insulting him with snide remarks, and not passing him the ball.

What happened to Rodney probably isn't unfamiliar to any of us. At some point in our lives, most of us have been subjected to what seemed like a true onslaught of contradictions that left us in the doldrums.

When a subject is confronted with a series of contradictory confirmations without being allowed to deal with any one of them, a scenario of *contradiction overload* takes place that habitually leaves its victim in psychological shambles. How did it all go so wrong for Rodney? Let's look back at what happened that day and see.

Rodney inadvertently had shown up in an entirely new environment that was frequented by a tightly knit group of similar-thinking individuals. Why was he welcomed by this group? Why did they let him play? Because, without realizing it, he'd offered these new players a golden opportunity to raise their

Contradiction overload is a term that describes a negative psychological state in which one experiences a repeated series of unresolved contradictions.

own self-esteem: he'd offered himself up as easy fodder for their own needs for neutralization! Rodney's sudden appearance was a fortuitous toy to play with; something to taunt and use as the group's little punching bag. Rodney's appearance on that court was a godsend, but not for Rodney. For Rodney, it was just the opposite and, quite logically, his psyche couldn't reconcile the illogical messaging that followed.

Rodney's level of control

In Chapter 2, I pointed out how being in control of our lives is a basic need we all share. Here, Rodney's total loss of control rendered him defenseless against the incessant contradictions that were doled out to him by his fellow players. As he made his way to the courts, he thought he knew exactly who he was and what he was capable of. There was nothing virtual about his self-image! He really was the star player on his former basketball team. But now that self-image had been called into question, and with it came self-doubt and serious damage to his self-esteem. His feelings of being in control were knocked out of his hands, and insecurity slid in to fill the void.

Can contradictions be controlled?

Because contradictions (negative relational confirmations) are unavoidable, it's simply not possible to always feel in control of contradiction and, therefore, our lives. Each one of us does our very best to regulate or control the contradictions we receive, as well as those we suspect await us. But life is full of surprises and sadly, they are often of the unpleasant kind. That said, just as with any other failed goal, should we just accept our plight in life and back down in defeat every time a contradiction appears? Can't we just take life's contradictions in stride and not let them affect us?

No, we can't! Relational contradiction and its emotional aftermath will always be experienced as damaging, and will always affect our thoughts, emotions, and conduct. Just as Rodney found out, not even trying harder is a guarantee of success.

So how can we arm ourselves against contradiction?

There are several ways of maintaining control over the contradictions we receive and that most of us are already familiar with. Acquiring a high level of notoriety or prestige is one way to smooth out many of life's rough spots. And of course, enriching ourselves monetarily can offer a major defense against many potentially contradicting circumstances. The problem is that these contradiction controllers aren't always easy to come by, and even under the best conditions still can't guarantee a turbulent-free journey. Besides, trying to control one's life to the nth degree is an exhausting and ultimately futile exercise. So, you might ask, is there any failsafe way to help defend ourselves against negative confirmations?

Yes, there is, and it takes the form of understanding. Understanding what actually causes us to think, feel, and behave the way we do can go a long, long way to helping us maintain our psychological equilibrium. I'm not implying that understanding how we are structured is some sort of panacea or silver bullet. And yet, understanding what causes the way we feel and behave is a giant first step toward turning trauma into triumph. After all, if you don't know how something works, there's little hope you'll be able to fix it (you and an equally knowledgeable therapist, that is).

Jackpot!

Emily was at the end of her single-mom rope as she waited in line at the checkout. Taylor, her youngest, was incessantly banging his little tootsies against the front of the cart, slowly eating away at Emily's patience. He'd stop when she told him to, but then start up again only moments later. The other two, Jenny and Janice, were currently missing altogether. Emily's eyes scanned the store as she put the groceries on the conveyor belt. Now what are they up to?

Ever since Paul up and left last year, it had been a struggle to put food on the table. This week she'd just squeak by. Her eyebrows lifted as she watched the twins lurk around the gumball machine trying to scam kind strangers out of their pocket change by looking as innocent and hungry as possible. How carefree it must feel to see a measly quarter as a major score!

Loading what she had bought into the cart, her eye noticed a lottery ticket dispenser that was positioned just in front of her. Normally she paid no attention to come-on's like that, but this time, being at the end of her rope, she fed a five-dollar bill into the slot, then navigated to the scratchers, and locked onto one that had four-leaf clovers and sparkly leprechauns all over it. It said the top prize was $100,000. She shook her head and smiled to herself. "What a joke!" She stuffed the card in her purse, yelled for the twins to come along, and made her way home. Emily pulled into her parking place and, like a zombie, made her way to the mailbox. Bills, an ad for hamburger meat, and some other worthless junk. Whatever happened to good old-fashioned mail? Was that even a thing anymore? After unloading the groceries and the stack of payback reminders, she took a moment to just sit down and catch her breath. Next, she'd conquer dinner. Then, almost haphazardly, she reached into her purse and brought out the lotto card, turned it over and thinking about what dinner might look like, did a little scratching. Pasta maybe? Symbols began to appear on her $5 purchase announcing each prize she hadn't won. She was starting to feel like an idiot.

Adios, $5! Then the final symbol appeared—a pot of gold—and it matched the one pegged as a winner! Suddenly, her dismay turned to shock. She couldn't move. Wanting the moment to last, she slowly, ever so slowly revealed her prize—$100,000! She took a deep breath. It would take her almost three years to earn that much money! She looked back at the prize amount, then, with arms spread wide, stood up with a jerk and began to skip around the kitchen twirling this way and that as she sung some unpublished song at the top of her lungs.

Financial gains can bring instant relief to potential contradictions

Most of us have been short on cash at one time or another. But Emily's shortage seemed eternal. That, and the obligation to feed three other mouths with no support from anyone were serious stress builders. Emily worrying about having enough money to cover groceries, not surprisingly, constituted a major contradiction for her. But now, suddenly, she could afford the things she needed. Her windfall gave her newfound control by giving her the power to eliminate many of the contradictions that would certainly be heading her way.

The rest of us, in the meantime, continue to face both positive and negative confirmations. Only now you're beginning to understand how these relationally confirming positive or negative echoes from our environment contribute to the way we think, feel, and behave.

The value of goal-getters

Certain needs or wants drive us to reach certain goals, and any object or service that can help us obtain those goals will have a special value. The more effective a contradiction combatant may be, the more value it will have. Sheer power over others can be considerably valuable for those who have it, and anything that can afford us such power, in any of its multiple shapes or forms, will always be welcome. As mentioned before, having substantial economic resources can calm our nerves almost to the point of complacency. There are also those products and services that can serve, quite effectively, as controllers of contradiction. The car we drive or cellphone we own, the right hammer, hair dryer, or dishwasher just when we need it, may have a special place in our hearts at a specific time in our lives, and yet, these human helpers are still limited in their capacity to deal with all of life's contradictions.

We all experience life both ***virtually*** (what we imagine is happening) and ***concretely*** (what we are convinced is real or truly taking place).

Virtual relationships increase the control we feel we have over our lives. Real relationships reduce that control.

It is logical that
living things
tend to contradict
the contradictions
they receive.

CHAPTER 5

Damage Control

Is there a better way to resolve life's persistent contradictions? Isn't there something one can do to get through this life with a little more affirmation, and a lot less conflict?

If, for example, we want to avoid future contradictions or repair contradictions that have already taken place, we have two basic options at our disposal: defense strategies and repair strategies.

- *Defense strategies* help us fend off contradictions before they can get off the ground.
- *Repair strategies* are designed to deal with contradictions, either in the precise moment they occur or in the future.

Sadly, in either case, positive results may not be easy to come by, and emotionally charged contradictions often may fester for years. (Humans hold grudges.)

Dealing with contradiction

When contradiction materializes and psychological damage occurs, our first logical tendency is to contradict the contradiction in an attempt to neutralize its damaging effects. You hit me, I hit you back. You insult me, I insult you. And so on. Neutralizations (a common repair strategy) come in all shapes and sizes. Keep an eye out for them. They're easily noticed. But above all, watch yourself. Watch how you react the next time somebody cuts you off in traffic, tells you "no" when you need to hear "yes," or instead of patting you on the back, degrades you.

Now that you're aware of how all of us deal with contradiction, when you find that someone is belligerent, rude, combative, insulting, or obnoxious, you will know that, for certain, he or she has fallen victim to contradiction, and is simply attempting to deal with its injurious effects. People don't lash out and become insulting or hard to get along with just because. They behave that way because they are reacting to a negative confirmation from their environment. It happens all the time.

The evolution of contradiction

Newborns react to contradiction from the time they're conceived. Once born, when they feel pain or sense a need they have that has not been satisfied, they will behave in exactly the same way adults do and act out with displeasure. The only difference between the reactions babies display and those of adults is caused by the limited resources babies have to express themselves. We adults can be sarcastic, harmful to others, wait for the right moment for revenge, or invent convoluted strategies to impede someone who is impeding us. Babies can only scream and cry, or cry, and then scream.

Neutralization is the most common contradiction repair strategy humans have at their disposal, and involves the largely unsuccessful practice of responding to a received contradiction with negation of that contradiction.

A subject's neutralization of an object's contradiction will invariably be felt by that object as just another contradiction.

Onward!

By this time, you've probably gathered enough information about The Structure that you're beginning to see how it can flex its muscles. You already know, for example, that it speaks directly to our need to be relationally involved with our environment. You've also seen that it demands that all relational activity be accompanied by some sort of awareness, echo, or confirmation of that activity. Additionally, you've seen that confirmations come in two varieties: positive and affirming, or negative and contradicting.

And finally, when it comes to confirmations, the positive ones often go unnoticed. But the negative ones almost never do. When who we are is thrown into question, denied, or sidestepped, a contradiction has appeared and we will react accordingly.

Contradiction and the real world

If you admire me, I will feel fulfilled. If you insult me, however, you may ruin my day. If your boss pats you on the back for a job well done, you may tell your friends about it at dinner. But if your boss criticizes you, you may complain about his poor judg-

No amount of mending can totally eliminate the damage some contradictions create.

ment. In short: Each relational interaction we have produces some sort of relationally created behavior.

This means that when Alfred contradicts Bruce, Bruce may feel prompted to contradict Alfred in an attempt to neutralize Alfred's contradiction. The problem with this scenario is that Alfred will then feel contradicted by Bruce, and very soon the stench of war may fill the air.

When we experience real contradictions—ones that take place in our concrete world—neutralizations are rarely effective. That said, in our virtual world (the fantasy world of our imagination), neutralizations usually fare much better.

Virtual victories ahead!

As just said, virtual neutralizations, more often than not, produce positive psychological results. This is because there is little danger that escalating, retaliatory consequences will follow. The virtual thinker usually has everything under control because it's their own imagination that is shaping the ensuing dynamic and its final outcome.

In our virtual worlds, we can effortlessly vanquish our enemies, forcing them to see their erred ways as they beg us for forgiveness. The virtual nature of our imaginations gives us the upper hand to direct events as we please. In our non-virtual worlds, however, our retaliatory goals often become a question of too little, too late. Had we only said this, then done that, our adversary surely would have seen how unreasonable they'd been and offered us their sincerest of apologies.

All in all, no matter what origin a contradiction may have, The Structure will invariably encourage its elimination. This doesn't mean that our efforts to do so will always be successful. It's a challenge to successfully neutralize the kind of damage some contradictions create. Indeed, attempts at doing so almost always turn into liabilities.

Rough patch

Gina's brain felt scrambled that morning. It had been feeling that way since the gal she'd thought was her best friend suddenly dumped her. Can someone really get thrown off a cliff just like that, especially by their best friend? How is that possible? When she'd been canned by guys it always stung, but this was different. She and her friend had been through so much together. Gina knew they hadn't been clicking lately, but she figured it was just a phase. And yet, Phyllis hadn't returned any of her calls or texts for weeks. As they say, no response is

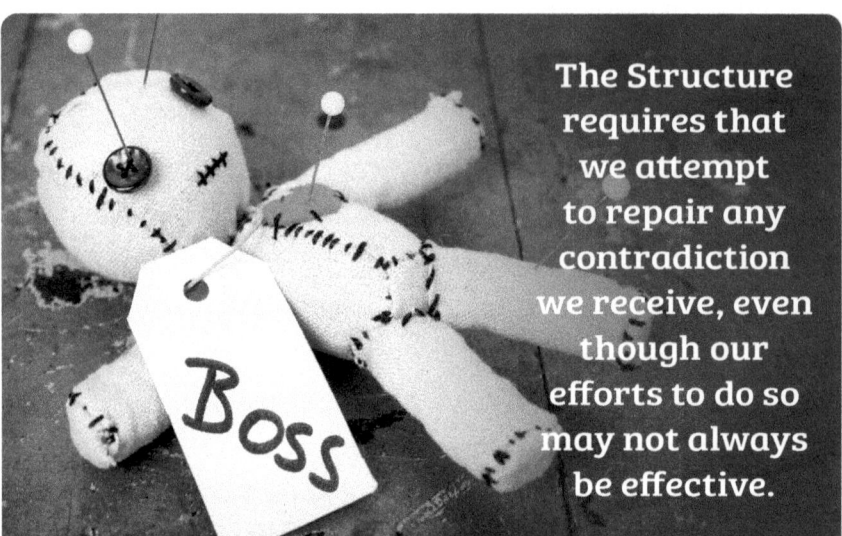

The Structure requires that we attempt to repair any contradiction we receive, even though our efforts to do so may not always be effective.

a response. Gina just didn't want to believe such a thing could actually happen and especially to her.

But right now Gina had to focus. She was at work, and when you're at work, you're supposed to be doing your job, not thinking about your personal life. She had a project to do, yet she continued to be distracted by her situation with Phyllis. She also knew Robert, her boss, gave her that project to do because she had always completed the jobs she'd been given. She was proud of the accolades she'd constantly received for her attention to detail and had gotten Employee of the Year twice! But this time around she'd already missed the deadline and was told she had until the end of the day to deliver, or there would be serious consequences.

As 5 o'clock approached Gina still hadn't turned in the report. She had every intention to do so, but her brain fog wouldn't lift. As she listened to the seconds ticking away on the clock hanging on the wall, she felt someone enter her cubicle. She slowly turned around in her chair. It was Robert. Her heart skipped a beat, and she felt perspiration forming on her upper lip. Her face was getting warm and she started to flush.

"Gina, I'm just not sure what to do here. I gave this one to you because it simply had to get done, on time. I've always been able to rely on you. But lately you seem to be slipping. Corporate is breathing down my neck. I don't know if I'm going to have to let you go..."

Gina couldn't believe what she was hearing. She was facing a major contradiction and wasn't sure how to handle it. Didn't Robert remember all the times she'd saved the day? She'd been his best employee for years! How could this man even suggest she was anything but valuable? But Robert's threats had reached Gina's soul, and The Structure just wouldn't let this one pass. Gina looked back at Robert. "How dare you accuse me of being anything less than exceptional? All those times I've saved your ass with corporate! And this is how I'm repaid? One little slip up and I'm gone?!" She knew she was right and was convinced Robert did too. She'd lost her composure, sure! But she knew he'd see things her way.

Robert shook his head and slowly backed out of her cubicle. "I'm surprised by you Gina. You've never shown this kind of disrespect. And all this seems especially out of place considering the situation. Please pack up your personal items. I'm sorry, but your employment here is over. You have fifteen minutes to vacate the building." And with that, Robert turned and walked away. Gina sat frozen to her chair as a member of security arrived to escort her from the building.

What just happened?

Gina saw herself as a generous, respectful go-getter who was always ready to help. But that particular day she was a wounded gazelle licking the psychological wounds she'd received from a best friend. And now this! As far as Gina was concerned, there was just as little fairness in Phyllis's behavior as there was in Robert's, and her attempts at neutralization had backfired. Apparently Gina fell into a depressive state, and trying to repair the damage from such severe contradictions had all the trappings of failing as well.

As Gina went over her situation, she realized that lately she really hadn't been herself and, in fact, hadn't actually turned in certain projects on time. But in Gina's mind that didn't make her a slacker. Slacking off never constituted one of Gina's goals; it had nothing whatsoever to do with her self-image. What her boss said to her directly contradicted the person she was convinced she was. That's the reason she reacted the way she did. Just like the rest of us, she was just following whatever directives The Structure demanded of her. She did her best to defend her behavior, but it just wasn't enough. Gina had already contradicted Robert, and now The Structure demanded that Robert balance things out in his favor, so that's what he did. Result: Nobody won anything. Everyone lost something.

All of us are consciously or subconsciously aware of who we are because we're equally aware of our needs and goals. That's why when someone or something contradicts one of those needs or goals, we feel compelled to put our lives back in logical order and do so in the quickest and most effective way possible.

The problem is that what might compensate one person's psychological standing can often throw someone else's out of kilter.

As we've already discussed, back-and-forth neutralizations often go amuck. In our next vignette, I'll illustrate how dynamic contradictions can develop, even under the most benign of circumstances.

Not very neighborly

"He's doing it again!" Walter yelled to Pam as he watched his neighbor, Ed, blow leaves in the direction of his precious koi pond. Walter took meticulous care of his entire yard, especially the Japanese-inspired garden that took him two years to construct. Pam rolled her eyes and decided to keep her mouth shut, silently wondering if this Cold War was ever going to end. Ed and Marsha had only lived next door for a few months, but it seemed like everything Ed did drove Walter bonkers. It really was too bad, because Marsha was a nice gal. Pam would have loved to have them over for dinner sometime. Clearly, that was out of the question, at least for the time being.

In a huff, Walter stomped to the garage and fired up his John Deere. As he mowed near the property line, he made sure to keep the rows on his side neat and tidy, but intentionally cut wavy patterns onto Ed's side as he mulched up the mess of leaves scattered about. He felt almost joyful as he lowered the blade and hacked away at Ed's Kentucky bluegrass, intent on causing as much damage as possible to the beautiful greens. Once he'd cut the area where the leaves had been blown, he pulled off

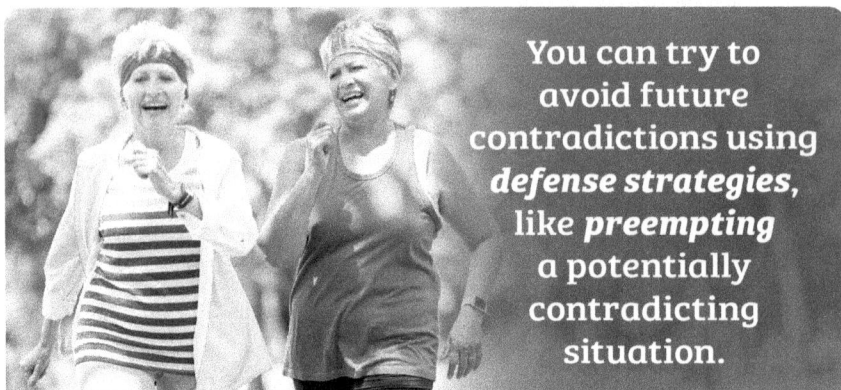

You can try to avoid future contradictions using *defense strategies*, like *preempting* a potentially contradicting situation.

the bag and marched it over to Ed's front door, where he proceeded to dump the contents all over the front stoop. "That'll send a message," Walter grumbled to himself, satisfied that the score was settled, and that would be that!

Marsha watched in horror as she saw what was happening. She knew that things were about to go from bad to worse. Since they'd moved in, Ed and Walter were like two little kids fighting over a toy. It was hard to believe they were grown men. She really liked Pam and wanted to keep her as a friend, even if the men wanted to blow up any chance of peaceful coexistence. So she texted Pam, asking her if she'd like to meet up for one of their walks. They had only done this a few times, but she was hoping they could make it a regular thing.

Pam met Marsha out at the street, and they started walking toward the park at the end of the block. "I am glad to have this chance to get to know each other better! It is so hard to make friends in a new place. How about we make a deal," offered Pam. "Whatever happens between the boys is between them. You and I don't have to play along."

Escalating contradictions

When people are at odds with one another, what follows can look like three-year-olds playing in a sandbox, only this time they're throwing metaphorical hand grenades at each other instead of sand or half-broken toys. One reaction leads to another; escalating contradictions emerge, and open conflict takes over.

Clearly Ed and Walter had been playing out this childish dynamic of theirs for months, one trying their best to neutralize the other's contradictions. Tit for tat. You hit me, I hit you, only harder. As far as understanding what had happened, the matter is simple: Contradictions most always have consequences.

When Walter saw that Ed had blown leaves into his yard, he felt contradicted by Ed's intentional assault, and compelled to even out Ed's affront. From Walter's point of view, this was the logical way to react and regain, for himself, some sense of vindication. But Ed, of course, saw things differently. Walter's obvious and logical re-establishing of justice for himself became a blatant injustice for Ed. As pointed out before, when one contradiction is served up to neutralize another, it often prompts a back-and-forth escalating exchange of negativity as each party vies for the upper hand. Ed may have known, on some level, that his leaf blowing had caused Walter distress, but as far as Ed was concerned, Walter deserved a little distress. This wasn't their first conflict. And based on both parties ignorance of how they are both structured, it was unlikely to be the last time they exchange neutralizations.

> The preset, mutually agreed upon rules commonly present in games allow contradictions to take place more virtually than concretely and, therefore, are not reacted to in the same way that real contradictions are.

A different approach

When someone is contradicted, they not only feel emotionally violated, but they also experience a loss of control, and rightfully so. If they had been in control, no contradiction would have taken place to begin with. Both Walter and Ed, for example, felt a loss of control at the hands of the other.

But Marsha and Pam were able to keep the relationship they had between themselves as neutral as possible. Since they were both well aware of this endless game their husbands were playing, they were able to mutually decide to stay out of the fray. From a structural point of view, they subconsciously chose a defense strategy called ***preempting***. It was clear to both wives that their husbands' bad behavior might continue, but by agreeing to not get involved, they were able to successfully mitigate any potential for contradictions between themselves. They still would have to deal with their husbands' drama, but now had considerably reduced any spillover effect that drama might have on their budding friendship. The wives intuitively preempted the real possibility of an escalation and, consequentially, shut down the contagious nature of the dynamic their husbands had created for themselves.

Can neutralization ever be effective?

By this time, you may be wondering if there are ever cases in which neutralizations actually work to deflate, deflect, or eliminate contradiction. The answer is yes, but such are either rare, virtual, or masquerade as simple challenges.

Games: a virtualization of life

As discussed, under normal conditions, only in virtual settings can contradictions be taken with a grain of salt and neutralizations be truly successful. Take games of all kinds and varieties, including all sports. Both are good examples of how certain kinds of contradiction can take place creating only measured amounts of psychological damage as a result. Sports are based on a mutual understanding between players that whatever occurs should be considered only virtual. Games are all about controlled contradictions; contradictions that take place according to a set of pre-established rules. In contrast, contradictions in real life are most always of the no-holds-barred variety. Where sports are involved, however, mutual agreed upon rules of engagement reign supreme making contradiction far more impersonal. When all else fails, blame the rule book.

Bar fight: the real world

John and Peter had been at each other's throats for some time. The original source of conflict was a woman—Peter had "stolen" John's girlfriend, Lorraine. Since then, every time they'd run into each other they would exchange sneers. As time went on their friends fed the animosity and both men became increasingly incensed when they would show up at the same place.

One evening at the local bar, John was carousing with his buddies when Peter's crew arrived. Ramon, John's right-hand man, gave him the alert. "Look who it is. You ought to do something about that prick." John agreed. It was time!

John moseyed over to Peter, leaned against him, and said, "You need to leave—now!"

"It's a free country. I'll go where I please," Peter snorted back, walked past John, and checked him with his shoulder as he made his way back to where his friends were loving the escalating tension.

As Peter walked away, John whipped around, grabbed Peter's shirttail and yanked him back, pulling the flannel off his shoulders. Peter immediately spun around and shoved his face inches from John's. "You think you're a tough guy? Lorraine already told me you're nothing, and she'd know!"

The ensuing brawl ended with John falling to the floor, panting and dizzy, face and fists covered in blood. His friends helped him to his feet and dragged him into the street to escape further attacks and humiliation. John

found a seat on a cement divider in the parking lot, in pain. As he licked his wounds, he began to ruminate on how he'd eventually vindicate himself! The Structure demanded it. No one can just leave a contradiction festering without plans to eventually neutralize it.

In contrast...

Boxing match: the virtual world

The western division's welterweight championship was underway. Matt Amari was the favorite, being undefeated in this, his senior year. Jerry Fang was going to give it all he had, but knew the odds were stacked against him. He was just hoping the match would go to a decision. A knockout would be hard to swallow. Not to mention how his head would hurt in the aftermath.

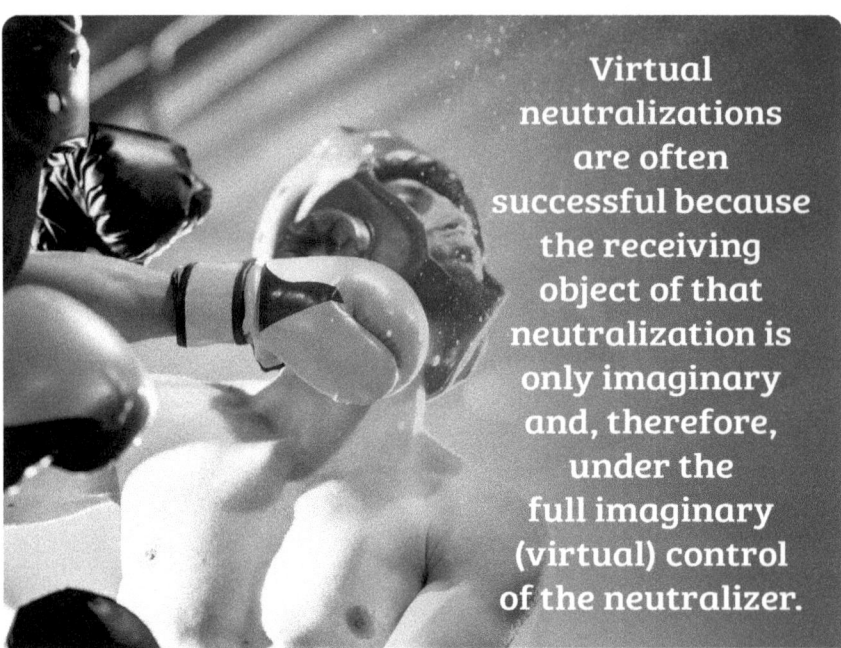

Virtual neutralizations are often successful because the receiving object of that neutralization is only imaginary and, therefore, under the full imaginary (virtual) control of the neutralizer.

By the time the third round arrived, Jerry was fatigued and having trouble holding his own. Matt landed a double-jab-cross combo, and quickly followed with an uppercut. Jerry fell to the floor. The referee went to a 10-count, and the match was over. Matt helped Jerry to his feet and the three stood aside one another in the center of the ring as the ref lifted Matt's glove, declaring the winner.

Boxing matches and other games

The above contentious encounter was jam-packed with contradictions and counter-contradictions, but because they were played out under a set of mutually agreed upon rules, (a scenario that never takes place in real life); none sparked true conflict;

none were taken too personally. It was only a game and, therefore, could be considered only virtual, not real or concrete.

Structurally speaking, confrontations like the previous one follow preestablished courses of action characterized by the environmentally controlled conditions under which those courses of action take place. Under such conditions, any negative impact a contradiction may produce is most often shared by all involved.

The psychological impacts that take place in certain individual sports, however, can be harder to emotionally disregard. In chess, squash, boxing, handball, fencing, or tennis, contradictions can be taken to heart more easily as there are no teammates to share contradictions with. Nevertheless, in spite of the more individual nature of such games, the mutually agreed upon rules of engagement place emerging contradictions into a more virtual-like plane thereby alleviating players and spectators alike from the rigors of having to deal with the emotional effects of conflict.

War movies, love stories, and virtual, life-like conflict

Watching movies or theater productions where serious conflict takes place, spectators are safely taken on a journey of mayhem and emotional ups and downs but whose consequences remain virtual. All involved, producers and spectators, understand that what's being shown is very much under control—a scenario that is sufficiently divorced from real life to keep participants reasonably safe from the damage true contradictions invariably create.

It's interesting to note, however, that in spite of the virtual nature of most games, many of us can still be emotionally impacted by certain virtual experiences. Just occasionally ask a game player how they felt about their latest defeat.

Gambling and contradiction

Games played where the exchange of money is added to the mix, however, cannot be considered all that virtual because they're not! The exchange of money instantly transforms virtuality into reality, often exchanging one's tears coming from a virtual relationship to tears emanating from true psychological pain.

Neutralizations can leave scars

In our real or non-virtual world, trying to repair (neutralize) damage created by contradictions rarely mitigates or stops contradictions from appearing in the first place. After centuries of being involved in this structural merry-go-round, few of us have learned that an ounce of prevention is worth a pound of cure. And yet, sure as can be, it can happen from time to time.

> Legal rulings can be effective neutralizers of contradiction because such rulings are shared by that environment of which the neutralized object forms an integral part.

Marsha and Pam's pact to protect themselves from their husbands' exchange of contradictions is a perfect case in point.

We should also take into account that, with the exception of contradictions of the virtual kind, most produce at least some degree of damage. In the end, no matter how effective or clever a repair job may be, no amount of mending can totally eliminate the damage some contradictions create. Something that's been repaired rarely ends up being in better shape than when it was damage-free.

Human justice, and The Structure that guides it

Now that you're beginning to understand how we're affected by the way we're structured, you'll better understand how most judicial systems are created, and why they are inherently doomed to rarely get it right.

Jurisprudence is created by one's social environment. When a series of rules made by a society are broken (contradicted), that society will move to neutralize any associated contradictions that occur. The high point of neutralizing contradictions through socially accepted norms and rules is that such neutralizations are sanctioned by the social environment itself, thereby leaving little doubt as to who has been vindicated and who hasn't. In a word, when it comes to environmentally sanctioned neutralizations, the buck stops at the judge's bench! There will be no subsequent escalations of conflict to deal with. The victory of the condemned or the innocent will be final, and its emotional stamp on those implied, definitive.

So why are all judicial systems as imperfect as they are? Human laws are designed to address but one specific kind of social contradiction, and *one* only. This means that, like a broken clock that's only correct two times a day, no law, norm, or ruling is 100 percent on its mark every time. As a matter of fact, laws can hit the nail on the head only every once in a while. This, because there are almost always mitigating circumstances to a crime committed that, were justice to be doled out with true fairness in mind, would either lead to a total acquittal or a moderated punishment.

Emotional responses of vindication

The other day on the news, I listened to a woman express her elation after hearing that the murderer of her child would spend the rest of his life behind bars. In a statement to the press, and as she choked back tears of joy, she declared that receiving the news of the perpetrator's sentence had gifted her the happiest day of her life.

How is it possible, one might ask, that a fellow human's demise can produce such elation in another? Just remember that the promise of a successful affirmation or neutralization can produce powerful emotions in us all. Fulfilling the mandates of The Structure that guide us can be, for some, life's cherry on top. How many novels, plays, or movies have pleased audiences over the centuries when they've dealt with definitively neutralizing an unjust contradiction. How triumphant it is when the evil shark, cruel dictator, school bully, or torturous prison warden, finally meets their just reward for being the unjustified, contradicting entities they are!

As far as a nation's judicial system is concerned, for example, one cannot expect a court's verdict to eliminate the pain of an unjust wrong, and yet any ensuing retributions can provide, sometimes, a significant degree of meaningful consolation to a victim or victims of injustice. Neutralizations, like those sanctioned by our social environment, are probably the only neutralizations that can truly satisfy our psychological need for fairness.

Strength in numbers

The tried-and-true adage "there is strength in numbers" is another psychological phenomenon that becomes more understandable when examined from a structural perspective.

Remember that how we are valued as individuals originates from our environment, not from ourselves. Consequentially, the larger the number of validations and validators an individual may have, the more psychologically powerful such validations will be.

For example, it doesn't have the same impact if Ada and Danny say they saw a UFO than when an entire town sees the same thing in the same place at the same time. The quantifiable number

Contradictions with origins that are shared by a large number of subjects are more effective than those that are initiated by a single individual.

of positive or negative points of relational echo count heavily when passing judgment on the validity of any given occurrence. We've all heard the expression, "Sixty-million Frenchmen can't be wrong!" or "But mommy, everybody's got one." Get enough people to say that something is true, bad, good, false, or valuable, and soon that's how that thing will be valued.

Understanding what actually causes us to think, feel, and behave the way we do can go a long, long way to helping us maintain our psychological equilibrium.

Relational
confirmation can
come from
either animate
or inanimate objects.

CHAPTER 6

An Introduction to Some of The Structure's Intricacies

It is worth noting that both relational confirmation as well as relational contradiction can be split into two separate categories: 1) animate and 2) inanimate. Animate contradictions come from things that are alive, like you and I are, while inanimate contradictions speak to those things that are not, like your car, or a can of soup. Interestingly, it's in the inanimate world that neutralization can, from time to time, work with reasonable success. For example, in previous vignettes we exclusively dealt with animate objects. Let's see now how conflict plays out when the adversary is an unwitting object.

The sticky pickle jar

Lindsey couldn't wait to get home. It had been a long week, so her Friday evening plans were simple—slap a few things together for dinner, then make a beeline for the sofa and crash in front of her new TV. As if she were being timed, Lindsey made herself a classic Italian sub, loaded the plate down with vinegar chips, then grabbed the pickle jar out of the fridge. She set the sandwich down on the table to concentrate on the jar, grabbed it firmly in both hands, and gave it a twist. Nothing! And this wasn't the first time.

Inanimate objects that can't be accessed, automatically contradict a person's needs and goals.

Lindsey tried again. Still nothing! The jar kept defying her goal of opening it. Straining and more straining led to the same nonstarter, and frustration began welling up inside her. Lindsey ran the lid under hot water, but that just made her hands slippery. Exasperated, she grabbed the handle of a knife and took a whack at one of the lid's sides. "POP!" And there it was! Lindsey successfully neutralized the jar's stubborn ways and let out a satisfying sigh of relief.

Inanimate neutralizations (and projection)

What does the pickle jar story tell us about ourselves? It tells us that it doesn't matter if an inanimate object is incapable of intention, emotion, or voluntary responses. Contradictions are contradictions no matter how they're packaged, and so are affirmations. They may emerge from the affirming actions of another living being, or a contradicting, unopenable pickle jar. It doesn't matter. Whatever the case may be, when we feel how our environment interacts with us, we will do so in living, breathing human terms. There is no other way we can experience the world around us. That's just the way we're structured.

The logical foundation of The Structure

Unlike the acrimony that contradiction can create between animate beings, Lindsey's inanimate pickle jar saga was far less damaging emotionally to her than Ed and Walter's feud or John and Peter's bar fight. When we are contradicted by an inanimate object, we have a better chance of successfully neutralizing its negative influence on our psyche. (Inanimate objects don't hold grudges, so continuing, back and forth neutralizations shouldn't be an issue.) And yet, as we know, just like all other objects in our environment, inanimate objects do form an integral part of our psychological standing.

Inanimate objects can deny or favor our goal-seeking ways, potentially becoming objects of affirmation (i.e., an unbreakable dam, an unsinkable boat, or a tool that has never failed us), or they also can contradict us (i.e., a door that won't shut, a jar that won't open, or a gun that won't fire). When inanimate objects appear to resist or, to the contrary, cooperate with our needs and goals, they can and should be experienced in human animate terms. (Life is an animate event.)

If, for example, your hammer hits your thumb instead of what you were planning to hit, you might throw it to the side in anger. Psycho-structurally speaking, your hammer contradicted you (one of your goals) and, therefore, according to The Structure, needed to be neutralized. What you wanted to do was to hit a nail square on its head, but that isn't what happened. The hammer failed to do its job and hit your thumb instead. Consequentially, and in order to meet the conditions of The Structure, you were obliged to manifest, in the most expressive way possible, that what had contradicted you had not behaved according to your wishes (who you were at the time). Such culpable objects or events can be almost anything that's part of who you considered yourself to be at the time, like a malfunctioning finger, brain, hand, eye, etc. In such cases, and, in order to neutralize whatever it was that contradicted you, all that's necessary is that you recognize who you are now as compared to that part of you that failed to properly carry out one of your needs or goals in the immediate past. For example, you could simply declare, "God, I'm dumb," "Stupid finger!" "I've got to have these legs looked at." "I wonder what's wrong with me. I used to be good at that."

A more important question is if, when we neutralize an inanimate object or event that forms a part of our relational orbit, is it because we have illogically animated that object or event then behaved illogically or, on the other hand, have we simply dealt with an inanimate object the way we do because it forms a part of who we animatedly are? If we are our environment

We often logically bestow human characteristics on those inanimate objects in our environment that provide us with significant relational confirmation.

and our environment is us, we have the very logical potential of experiencing our inanimate world for what it is: a part of who we animatedly are. What sense would it make if we were to experience relationally interacting inanimate objects in any other way?

More on our inanimate world and projection

In classical psychology, it's thought that when someone perceives their own state of mind as belonging to others, they do so in order to protect their egos from damaging subconscious content. But what are we trying to hide or suppress from ourselves when we feel elated and, subsequently, experience the world around us as equally joyous?

When we swear at a door that won't close or are angered by a jar that won't open, are we attempting to protect ourselves from some personal shortcoming, or are we simply trying to neutralize a common environmental contradiction? Again, if our environment forms an essential part of who we are, and we form an essential part of our environment, isn't it only logical that we perceive our environment the same way we perceive ourselves: in animated human terms?

You may remember Tom Hanks' friend Wilson, a volleyball in the classic film *Cast Away*. Wilson was the only object that remained from the plane crash Tom had fallen victim to, and that had left him stranded on an uninhabited South Pacific island. Wilson became Tom's best friend while he was on that island. But was that because Tom needed to protect his inner self by projecting some unwanted subconscious content onto an inanimate volleyball? Or was it simply that Wilson, the volleyball, was the only familiar object left in Tom's environment that was structurally meaningful to him? Since the world around

> Behaviors often labeled
> as "defense mechanisms" are
> nothing more than our
> logical attempt at neutralizing
> a contradiction.

us, animate or inanimate, is what allows us to remain physically and psychologically alive, logically we will sense that world as life-giving and therefore, as relationally vital to us as might be any other thing, living or not.

For example, if the only objects on planet Earth were you and a single gray rock, your life would be psychologically dependent on that rock, and you'd be interacting with it all day long. You would behave this way not because you were irrationally projecting some unwanted subconscious content outside of yourself and onto some inanimate gray lump of random matter, but rather because that's the way all living things must *relate* to their relationally based environments. Any object or event that is experienced as *life-giving*, will equally be experienced as *lifelike*, and any object or event that is *lifelike*, will be experienced as *life-giving*.

Following this same rational equation, note that we name boats after people and refer to them as "she," complement our tools when they perform as expected, praise a water dike for holding up in a flood, or silently thank an airplane for staying together in heavy turbulence. We do this not to defend ourselves from any potentially harmful emotions but rather because that's the way we (and everyone else) are logically structured.

Humans want nothing to do with error

When a tennis player makes a bad shot, you'll often see them straighten out the gut on their racket as if the gut had something to do with the mistake they just made. A football player might check his cleats or tweak the position of his helmet. A golfer, pick a different club, and a competitive swimmer, adjust their swimsuit in preparation for a faster lap next time. These behaviors are not created by some subconscious mechanism that mysteriously expunges painful feelings outside of ourselves. There is no such thing as psychological mechanism. There is only psychological logic. No amount of so-called projection has ever protected anyone from anything.

Offensive inanimate objects

As far as actions emerging from our inanimate world are concerned, there are cases in which some contradictory inanimate events can produce emotional responses with equal or more intensity than any animate event might. A gun might jam when one's life is in danger, a window might not open when there's a fire, or a cell phone may not turn on when you need urgent help. Other factors can also make an inanimate object surprisingly offensive, like when Walter dumped leaves all over Ed's doorstep. Here, we know the leaves didn't get there all on their own, but still, their presence sent a very clear message to Ed, and it wasn't an affirming one.

In the case of the pickle jar that refused to open, a tool was used to successfully neutralize the jar's contradiction. Nevertheless, a real contradiction did take place when the jar wouldn't open, and the negative impact of that contradiction affected Lindsey's psyche. All contradictions have psychological consequences. And yet, as we know, very few acts of neutralization succeed in fixing much of anything, often provoking, instead, a negative chain reaction of continuing, give-and-take contradictions.

Sticky jar (alternate ending)

Lindsey gave herself a little pep talk to pump her up enough to loosen the lid, but no dice. At this point, she was growling to herself. She was frustrated and could feel a trace of anger start to well up inside her. She just wanted to be on to the part where she got to veg out on the sofa. Instead, she was getting a forearm work-out, straining, then straining some more to no avail. She needed a better grip, so she grabbed that silicone thingy that would help her gain traction. Still, no luck. She ran the lid under hot water. Nothing! Exasperated, she grabbed a knife and started whacking the back of the jar. Nothing moved. By this time Lindsey's anger had reached fever pitch, and in a moment of total frustration, she wailed the jar against the tile floor and voilà, the jar was finally open! Feelings of victorious relief, however, were quickly replaced by remorse as Lindsey realized that the pickles she so wanted to eat had been impaled by shards of broken glass on the dirty floor.

Unsuccessful neutralizations feel like failures

Lindsey's smacking of the jar against the floor and breaking it into a thousand pieces was, as it turned out, not the most satisfactory way to neutralize the jar's contradictory behavior. Although she had an initial feeling of victory when the jar finally broke open, it provided only a temporary sense of closure, a sense that was quickly replaced by feelings of defeat. As so often happens in cases like this, contradictions can often backfire, prompting us, in the future, to find more appropriate ways of dealing with contradiction's destructive nature.

To neutralize, or not to neutralize

All humans implicitly try to neutralize, at least to some degree, every contradiction they're confronted with, be it virtually (we make up a story in our heads that culminates in a successful neutralization), or we directly deal with the contradiction itself, and become more explicit about the way we vindicate ourselves. Regardless of the chosen tactic, all neutralizations begin with us demonstrating rejection of whatever it is that's contradicting us. This, The Structure demands we do in order to demonstratively verify to ourselves and others that we are no longer associated with the contradiction itself. We can't be. We're logical beings, and contradiction is logic's diametric opposite.

At the first sign of contradiction, we enter rejection mode, a behavior in which we reject whatever it is that is contradicting us. Next, we attempt to neutralize, in one way or another, the painful effects of the contradiction itself. This, even though neutralizations rarely lead to satisfying results, and the reason why most experienced humans often limit themselves to simply manifesting their disassociation from the contradicting object or event, and leave it at that. For example, when faced with a contradiction, we might make a facial expression that shows our relational detachment from its illogical nature. Sometimes a simple shake of the head or curt expression of disapproval is enough to get our point across and afford us some degree of relief.

Tools of the trade

Neutralization is not the only means we have at our disposal when dealing with contradiction. Another useful tactic is ***compensation***. For example, when someone is not able to complete a certain task when they are expected to (acquire a degree, build a shed, become a major influencer, own a successful company, etc.) they will often anticipate that an explicit contradiction may not be far off and try and sidestep that eventuality. This, they may do by directing their efforts toward becoming successful in some other personal endeavor of similar environmental value, only this time, on their own terms.

Dean's List

Asher knew that's all his parents cared about. How many times had he heard them brag about his older sister making the Dean's List? Like, every semester? It was easy for her. Well, not easy in the sense that she didn't have to work at it. The trick was that it came naturally to her. And it wasn't like he was a total screwup. I mean, he'd made it into the same school that she did, after all. His grades weren't quite as good, but they were good enough. Why couldn't they just be happy with that?

Compensation is a typical defense strategy humans adopt to help prevent a likely contradiction by creating a similar behavior, only this time, on their own terms.

"You're not working up to your full potential," was the denouncement his mom and dad chanted every time his report card arrived. "You could be getting all A's. Like your sister. Why don't you apply yourself?" As if getting good grades was all life was about. Asher saw it differently. He wanted more freedom to do as he pleased. He did what needed to be done, but never wanted to go that extra mile. It was his life, after all. Why couldn't his parents just accept that?

In order to compensate for the slacking he'd done in his first few of years in college, he decided to take an intensive Spanish course over the summer. (Take note: that was Asher's idea, and he would tackle that challenge on his own terms.) This would get him the 12 foreign language credits he needed to graduate and would counter a common parental question: "Stephanie graduated in just seven semesters—magna cum laude! How about you?"

This is why Asher decided to go for the Dean's List during the summer. Maybe with a little more effort he could get them off his back.

Asher got top scores in all three levels of Spanish and was awarded that previously elusive Dean's List distinction. "Congratulations!" his mom exclaimed, but in her very next breath wanted to know why her son couldn't have been getting grades like that all along?

Compensating like a champ!

Asher wanted to avoid the predictable disappointment (contradiction) his parents, like clockwork, would express semester after semester at what they deemed inadequate scholastic performance. Asher was, by nature, not driven to excel in school. But by overcoming his predisposition to be a lazy student, he managed to gain approval (affirmation) from his parents. Here we can see how compensation can be an effective replacement for neutralization.

Are all compensatory behaviors as successfully authentic as Asher's? (Asher truly enjoyed his Spanish classes and felt genuinely gratified learning the language.) No, they're not, nor is one's relationship with such behaviors necessarily long lasting. It's hard to keep up inauthentic behavioral facades. None of us like to fake our way through life. The very notion repels us just as much as do the contradictions we're trying to compensate for. But that was not what Asher did. Asher's interest was as real, authentic, and satisfying for him as it is for many who find this tactic a rewarding way to live their lives. Once one can do something "their way," new, exciting relational vistas can open and profoundly nourishing opportunities for affirmation can make themselves known.

Compensation and becoming a new you!

There is no question about it. Compensation requires changes in one's behavior. This is precisely what Asher did when he buckled down at summer school. In the end, his newfound stick-to-it-iveness not only helped squelch any future contradictions but helped make up for (neutralize) some of Asher's accumulated contradictions of the past.

Once again, keep in mind that strategies of compensation are only successful when carried out on the compensator's own terms. That is to say, not as dictated by someone else, but as self-ordained by the compensator themselves. The compensator remains the subject of his or her actions and this, as we're about to learn, is important. As long as whoever is making up for lost time or lost triumphs remains the true, indisputable subject of their actions, all will go well. It's when an action by one subject is inauthentic that relational red flags go up and barriers to success are quickly put into place.

Changes in one's behavior and relational authenticity

The difference between trying to become someone we're not (which of course is futile), or simply producing the kind of behavior that is more acceptable to our environment can, at times, be indistinguishable. For this reason, frequently those who compensate for what they perceive as a personal inadequacy may occasionally sense self-doubt about their true selves; a situation, nevertheless, that is frequently resolved when the doubting subject realizes how much authentic enrichment their new behavior has brought them.

Can compensation backfire?

It isn't so much that compensation can backfire but rather how compensatory behavior can create certain behaviors we won't see in those who don't practice it. You may notice, for example, how those who sense that their behavior is driven by environmental factors instead of genetic ones are, sometimes, inclined to clear *their* air and come clean to themselves and others. An indication of this is when you hear someone say, "I know I look pretty good out there, but I'm really just a phony," or "You see me working 24/7, but I'm one of the laziest people on Earth," or "You'd think I love to spend my day cleaning everything, but if I had my way, I'd never lift a finger." These individuals are more sensitive about having themselves and/or others detect some level relational inauthenticity about their person and call them out on it. Admitting to a bit of skullduggery helps such individuals to maintain their own relational integrity. All in all, most of us feel it necessary to be honest with ourselves and, therefore, with our environment, at least as long as we experience our environment as being honest with us. When we don't, however, all bets are off.

Control and preemption

Another structured defense strategy, ***preemption***, is often used to fend off contradictions that may be on the horizon. In these cases, the possible victim will get ahead of the game and attempt to extinguish any salvo of negativity possibly coming their way. This they do by demonstrating the control they have

Preemption helps prevent future contradictions
by demonstrating to one's environment
the control they wield over their own life.

over their lives before the subject is even brought up. For example, one might announce that they are perfectly aware of what is transpiring around them. They might announce to their surroundings, for example, that they're totally familiar with their limits and flaws—nothing catches them by surprise! "I don't really know much about this but if you're looking for some free advice...," or "I never got the memo, but I'll still give this thing a try." Or, "This might sound stupid but..." Through preemption, individuals are able to demonstrate to a potentially contradicting environment that they are in perfect control of their lives and not in need of being set straight via more contradiction.

In Asher's case, he had been feeling anxious as finals approached. Consequentially, by saying: "I always choke at finals," he positioned himself ahead of being accused (contradicted) of having lost control over his studies. In this way, were he to fail the exam, he would have still demonstrated to himself and others that, no matter what, he wouldn't be blindsided by the result of his efforts, thereby reducing the impact of any impending contradiction.

In similar situations you will notice people making a special effort to let others know that they have the reins of life firmly in hand. "I knew that was going to happen," "I thought you were going to say that," "That almost always happens," or simply, "Who said life was fair?"

Keep your eyes and ears open and you will begin to notice how many times others use this type of defense strategy in an effort to keep their selves as far from contradiction as possible. For example, you may hear someone quip, "I can help you paint that shed, but I'm not very good with a brush," "I'll take the exam, but I never opened the book" or "I don't want what I'm about to say to scare you, but...," and so on. Behaviors like this throw up universally effective contradiction barriers that can do wonders to take the punch out of any possible future negative environmental confirmations.

Modifying our goals

In another anti-contradiction tactic, if we suspect that a future contradiction is in the cards, we might modify the nature of the goals we set for ourselves. For example, Jimmy Jr. might want to ask for $20 to shovel snow from his neighbor's driveway, but fearing his neighbor might reject his offer (contradict him), he only asks for $15. Or someone might think, "I'd like to ask Ted out for lunch, but he might say no so I'll just walk with him for a while." Or "My boss expects me to ask for a three-week vacation, but I'll make it two just in case." (Just in case he comes back with a big, fat contradicting, "NO!")

The absence of control

It bears mentioning that, sometimes, potentially contradictory situations are given a free shield of protection simply because there exists a socially acceptable condition that lifts the responsibility of one's actions from environmental competence. Like how the blind are forgiven for running into things. Tone-deaf folks on karaoke night aren't expected to participate. Someone with a physical disability will get a free pass for not exercising, and game spectators, across-the-board permission to yell and scream uncontrollably.

Out-of-control, and loving it

More significant still are those relational activities that are automatically freed from environmental judgment, like allowing those who have fallen in love to pay attention to no one else but themselves. The specific act of consuming food and drink (not necessarily its aftermath, however) is, in and of itself, judgment-free and, therefore, universally accepted as ok to do however and whenever a subject feels it necessary. Releasing all control over one's reactions during a rock concert or comedy show, engaging in sexual activity, or any behavior that might emerge from contemplating beauty are also pathways of affirmation commonly considered free from potential contradiction and, for this very reason, universally sought after. All in all, as is structurally logical, affirmations that come directly from "non-judgmental" (non-contradicting) relationships are some of humanity's most coveted, often serving as go-to or fallback activities that reassure us that we belong in this world.

By modifying our goals to become more easily attainable, we can reduce any potentially contradicting barriers.

Environments set the rules, determine morality, and tell us what's right and wrong

In Ecuador, Madagascar, or Guatemala not being tall is an expected physical trait. There, tall people are often regarded as unusual, even threatening. To the contrary, in other countries, being short is viewed in opposite terms. In some societies having dark skin is the accepted norm; in others, it might generate suspicion. In one environment it's the right thing to do to wear a hat at church; in another, it isn't. In a word, one nation's or group's "right" may be another nation or group's "wrong."

Contradiction, a common human condition

The previous examples are just a brief sampling of some of the ways society (the environment) determines what is contradictory and what isn't. Any experience we have that conflicts

with, contradicts, or denies any living thing's needs or goals will always be unacceptable. But what happens when we lack the practice, resolve, or resources to battle contradiction in the first place? Perhaps we're missing the confidence or courage to stand up for ourselves, or think we must summon our inner Buddha so that not even the worst of contradictions bother us. Is it possible that we can find ways of not letting the slings and arrows of life influence then control how we think, feel, and behave? Yes it is, and centers around understanding; understanding how it is that we are structured and why it is we behave the way we do. Briefly stated, understanding how we are structured can enable us to deal with the illogical relationships life consistently confronts us with—and be better people for doing so.

Changes of venue

When we find ourselves having to constantly absorb relentless contradictions that come exclusively from the environment we live in, there are surrogate environments we can relate to that can provide the kind of affirming support we need to get on

> **Our environment (the society we live in) determines the "rules" of behavior (i.e., what is acceptable and what will result in a contradiction); changing one's environment may modify the chances of contradiction.**

with our lives. When who we are does not coincide with a specific environment's values, norms, and directives, changing that environment can smooth out life's hurdles in surprising ways.

But be on the lookout. With the exception of such aforementioned behavior-changing scenarios, trying to ignore the contradictions we receive but are unable to neutralize doesn't make them magically disappear. Indeed, one's accumulated contradictions end up forming an unwanted pile of un-dealt-with negativity, or a condition I call *contradiction overload,* a relational scenario that is as common as Friday night traffic or omelets made of eggs.

Contradiction overload and projection

In Chapter 4, Rodney, our unseated basketball star, experienced a case of contradiction overload that seriously compromised his emotional state. Those who suffer from similar situations will often view their environments exactly as they have been experienced: accusatory, critical, disparaging, and intolerant. Those who suffer from contradiction overload have not lost their minds, slid from reality, or unjustly become paranoid. They are simply victims of the negative, yet-to-be neutralized accumulation of illogical contradiction.

A contradiction overloaded individual will and should sense the world around them exactly the way they experienced it: menacing, difficult, vindictive, and unforgiving. In such cases they are not projecting anything from their selves outward into a world that doesn't deserve to be regarded as such. They are simply sensing their environment exactly as they experienced it. Take note, however, that even those cases in which an individual is genetically disposed to experience the world around them as menacing, harmful, or directly contradictory, they haven't twisted reality, as what they experience truly does take on those characteristics, albeit for them and them alone. There really are those of us that are born with "a chip on their shoulder." Remember, our self-images are the direct reflection of who we have become and continue becoming, environmentally. Relating to our environment is the only way we can acquire a self. We have no other choice; it's not anyone's particular fault that we think, feel, and react the way we do to our life's experiences. How can we blame a blind man for not being able to see, or penguin for its inability to fly. If any *one* or any *thing* is to take the rap for human behavior, it is The Structure itself, and nothing else.

To sum up how to better understand what has been tradition-ally labeled "paranoid behavior" keep in mind that we are our environment and our environment is us. Consequentially, when we hear someone comment, "I think those people over there are talking trash about me," we are not observing manifestations of illogical madness. We are observing a subject's just reaction to an environment they have concretely, virtually, or genetically experienced as threating, accusatory, or simply contradictory.

A multi-contradiction pile-up

Lately, Mandie had been having a rough time with her aging mother's ever-increasing forgetfulness. What had started as a few random "senior moments" had quickly turned into 24/7 dementia, and Mandie's brother and sister weren't being any help at all. They both lived too far away and were far too wrapped up in their own lives to lend a hand with their mother's care. Mandie understood, but found it frustrating that her wealthy brother hadn't offered to take care of at least some of her extra expenses, but so far, no offers had been made. Then, as she was getting ready to leave that morning, and right in the middle of her shower, the hot water heater burst, and her shower went from warm to ice cold. Now there was emergency cleanup to do and another expense she wasn't prepared for. And Barb was anything but understanding. She acted like Mandie was complaining about something just to annoy Barb. But what was Mandie supposed to do, start a fight with Barb? Mandie was the landlord, so whatever happened in that house was Mandie's responsibility, period.

Then, as if the day wasn't already going badly enough, now she was sitting on a freeway parking lot of frustration. Why wasn't anybody moving? She was going to be late for work…again!

> Then, all of a sudden, traffic started to slowly flow again, only just at that moment, a homeless man appeared slowly crossing in front of her car, and that did it! She'd hit her limit, rolled down her window and spat out a barrage of four-letter insults that must have left the poor man totally confused. Now what had he done?

Contradiction overload and the emotion of hate

Thanks to The Structure, when an opportunity for neutralization appears, we usually seize it. Be observant of your surroundings and you'll see what I mean. The next time someone inexplicably admonishes you (or someone else) with more intensity than you feel is deserved, realize that they may actually be yelling at their heavy-handed boss who treated them unfairly four hours earlier, a corrupt political figure that's been getting away with murder, or a loan officer who, only hours before, refused to save them from bankruptcy.

There are all kinds of ways we humans deal with contradiction, especially when we suffer from its accumulation. Interestingly, one of the most typical responses to pileups of negativity is the emergence of hate or loathing. As it turns out, this particular emotion serves as an extraordinarily effective contradiction neutralizer all by itself, hence the expression "love to hate." It can feel good to hate the perpetrator of a contradiction or series of contradictions. When we hate, we vent (neutralize) pent-up, accumulated frustrations, and find psychological solace doing so.

Hate is often utilized to neutralize all manner of contradictions.

Hate: a sure sign of contradiction

Notice how often we seek opportunities to express our disgust, repulsion, rejection, or animosity for what we sense are unjustified contradictions. What with instant global news and real-time transmission of data via social media, our relational worlds are rife with information we can use as hate generators.

For example, scrolling through rant after rant on social media we can easily find something or someone to feel disdain for, and in this way, check a few random items off our "neutralizations-to-do list." Surfing TikTok, Instagram, X, or any number of other social platforms, we can find a plethora of despicable, strange, inappropriate, or abhorrent people or events to virtually neutralize and bring us a little relief from our own home-grown woes.

In addition, when there is a numerically important number of us who hate the same thing, all that hating can pack a more significant recuperative punch than can just one person hating something or someone all by their lonesome. Remember, there's strength in numbers, especially when we're talking in psychological terms. That's why group therapy and support groups can, at times, be more effective than one-on-one sessions with a therapist.

Contradiction can get stuck on play and repeat

Remember those times you've found yourself continuously thinking about the same unresolvable conundrum? Of course you do. Just so you know, it's all about The Structure being hard at work trying to rid you of the distress you're feeling. Unfortunately, contradictions are rarely erasable from our psyches, and only those that are dealt with through understanding can be treated successfully. In the meantime, and under such conditions, The Structure will implicitly search for solutions to neutralize the contradictions received and, in the meantime, loop into an eternal *Groundhog Day* scenario of ineffective vindication.

Just know that this dynamic has always formed an essential part of the human condition in general yet, in the past, led theorists to speculate that humans may be genetically aggressive. But this makes no structural sense. If someone has an aggressive, rebellious, or vindictive tinge to their personality, that trait or tendency will either be spawned by their genetic background or by the accumulation of contradicting experiences.

Abandonment issues

"Why can't I just let it go?" Ainsley wondered aloud, even though she was alone in her apartment. She knew Tina hadn't meant to insult her. She probably wasn't even aware that her friend was feeling sensitive about her divorce. So many people have had failed marriages; it's a common situation.

So she decided to give Tina a call. Would Tina get defensive like she always did? "Hello?" Tina always answered the phone like she didn't know who it was, even though her screen had already given away the secret. "Hey, Tina! It's me. I just wanted to talk about the conversation we had yesterday." Ainsley's stomach knotted up. She hated confrontation.

Unneutralized contradictions will affect our psychological wellbeing unless and until they are dealt with.

"It's hard for me to say this, but you really hurt my feelings yesterday. I know you're sick of me talking about it, but when you suggested I just get over the breakup and move on, like I could just snap my fingers and make all that go away, it made me feel all alone. You're supposed to be my best friend. But lately it seems like you just want me to be somebody I'm not."

Tina felt blindsided. She had been there for her friend over and over, yet she was sick-to-death of hearing about Ainsley's jerk of an ex-husband! Why couldn't Ainsley just realize he did her a favor by leaving? She never meant to hurt her friend and could feel an indignant and defensive justification welling to the surface. But then she stopped to think. She and Ainsley were both suffering at the hands of the same contradiction.

Ainsley anxiously waited for her friend's reply. And for a moment, she wondered if the call had dropped or if Tina had already hung up on her. But then Tina said, "I am really sorry, Ainsley. I never meant to offend you like that. You're my best friend. I only want what's best for you. I should have realized you weren't ready to hear what I had to say. I should've just listened to you and not blabbed out my opinions like they are the only logical option. Can you forgive me?"

Ainsley broke into tears from relief. She was overjoyed to hear her friend acknowledge that she may have overstepped her boundaries and immediately realized that she, too, had been holding stubbornly to her own point of view.

Look before you leap

Ainsley alleviated her conflicted feelings by recognizing the painful nature of the mutual contradictions she had been feeling. As a result, instead of perpetuating the conflict, Tina was able to recognize the structural dynamic in which they were both involved and ultimately, a resolution was reached.

Alternatives to escalating contradictions

Mutually recognizing and then openly discussing the harmful characteristics of a jointly experienced contradiction can quickly lead to that contradiction being neutralized. Once both parties realize that both have suffered at the hands of a mutual contradiction, the contradiction reaches a point of neutrality, loses its contradictory character, and ultimately dissipates.

The Structure that guides us is built from three logical imperatives: *relationability*, *confirmation*, and *continuance*.

CHAPTER 7

The Structure's Structure

Hopefully these first few chapters have helped you to understand how our relational activity forms the behavioral basis of the lives we live. Indeed, the requirement that all living things be relationally active forms the primary imperative of The Structure we live by. Relational activity begins at conception when we start relating to the environment we were conceived in: the confines of our mother's womb. In addition, we don't emerge as clean slates of nothingness, waiting to be molded by the world around us. That was what thinkers like Jean-Jacque Rousseau and John Locke thought back in the 1700s, but now we know better. In fact, we're born already ladened down with surprising amounts of genetic baggage, baggage that contains a laundry list of specific physical and psychological traits that will manifest themselves as they're brought to life by their environmental surroundings.

For nine months, slowly but surely, our environment does everything it can to make sure we successfully transition from the carefree, protected confines we've grown accustomed to into the sensation-filled universe that will become our home until we take our last breath.

At birth, everything is brand new. For most of us, our five senses are all operational, yet we still have no idea whatsoever what's taking place around us, nor do we care. True cognition is on its way, but will take some time to fully kick in.

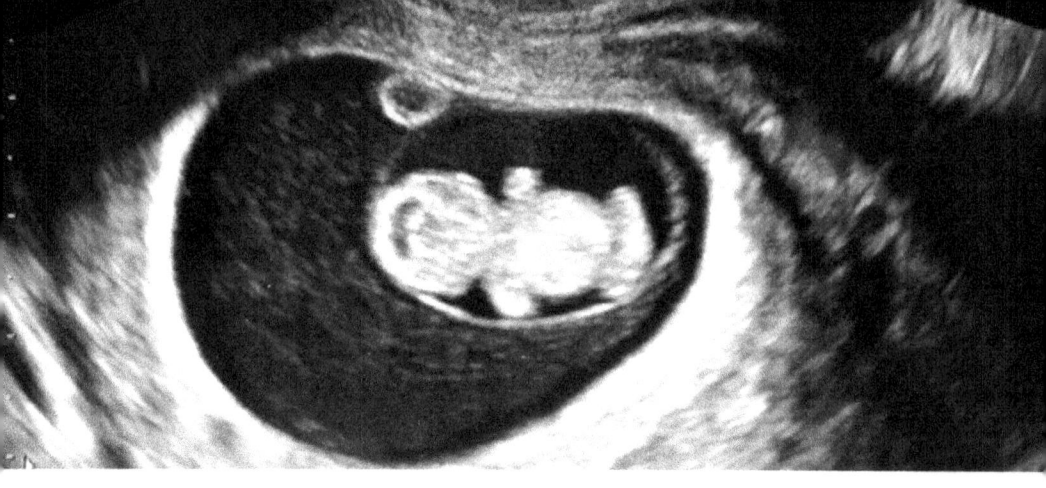

The Structure comes to life

The Structure that oversees the physical and psychological maturation all newborns are about to go through is built from three basic imperatives. As already discussed, the first is our need to be in constant relationship with the world around us or, if you wish, our environment. Relate or perish, as it were.

The second imperative outlines our need to continue existing, as non-continuation would be untenable. Either all living things continue relating or they can't exist at all.

The third structural imperative states that all relationships receive confirmation of the relational activity they're involved in. If no confirmational echo is forthcoming from a relationship, it cannot be said that a relationship has taken place.

The Structure that awaits us at conception is based entirely on the logical requirements of existence itself: *relationability*, *continuance*, and *confirmation*. These are the three imperatives of existence that all living things are bound to and are entirely responsible for everything we think, feel, and do.

In a nutshell, human behavior results from the imperative human need for us to be who we are. In over-simplistic terms, if the world around us (our environment) confirms our needs

> # One's relational activity begins at conception.

and goals, life is good, and we will behave in ways that positively reflect that fact. To the contrary, when a relationship denies one or more of our needs and goals (who we are), we will sense the presence of contradiction, and our behavior will manifest itself in equally contradictory ways.

Logically illogical

No matter how life goes down, for better or worse, every relationship we engage in contributes to our psychological status. Unfortunately, as we've come to learn, there are times when, instead of having who we are confirmed by a cooperative environment, the opposite occurs, and we find ourselves face-to-face with contradiction instead of affirmation.

As you have already heard me say several times, we humans are unexpectedly logical beings, a fact that emerges simply because that's how all existence, and therefore, all existing things, are structured. What one should surmise from this isn't that human behavior itself is necessarily logical, because it rarely is! What is being said, however, is that the fundamental cause of the way we conduct our lives is just as logical as $1 + 1 = 2$.

Let's imagine, for example, that Charlotte's father just contradicted a goal she had by telling her she can't go to a girls'

Humans are logical beings, as required
by The Structure, yet human behavior
can often appear to be quite illogical;
unexpected behavior is, nevertheless,
still the result of a logical catalyst.

night out party. As a result, Charlotte reacts in an illogical way. "Honey, Charlotte just turned all the lights out in her room and is hiding under the bed." To Charlotte, her reaction to her parent's contradiction was anything but illogical, even though the way she reacted might baffle most.

Realize that if Charlotte hadn't been at home when she was told that she couldn't go to that party, but rather at her local pharmacy, she surely would have reacted in a completely different way than how she did protected by the privacy of her own room. When we have a better option to express the way we feel about something, we'll adjust our reactive behavior accordingly. When we don't, we'll attenuate our reaction.

Is The Structure bulletproof?

Many ask if we would still live by the same Structure if, perhaps due to the influence of drugs, physical trauma, surgery, or some other invasive event, the brain itself were damaged or altered in any way.

The answer to that question is yes. The Structure is essentially bulletproof as it is comprised of imperatives that allow all existence to be what it is, no matter the conditions under which it manifests itself. No matter what state an existing thing may be in it will always behave according to the existential imperatives that guide the behavior of all existing things.

The missing link—continuance

In addition to our insatiable need for relational recognition, be it virtual or concrete, all relational activity demands we form an air-tight bond with our future—even if that future feels uncertain or threating. Every positive or negative, constructive or destructive encounter we have with the outside world (every confirmation, be it positive or negative) helps us complete The Structure's third relational mandate: *continuance*.

The continuation of our relational activity (our future) is a structural necessity that can be easily overlooked yet remains as essential to our lives as do The Structure's other two vital imperatives: relational activity and relational confirmation. Continuance is so vital to us that, just like the other two structural priorities, without a clear perception of our future, our lives would come to an abrupt end and stay that way.

Take note, for example, how we are drawn to things that are new, like the news itself. (The term news is simply plural for the word new.) Newness announces continuance: a new thing to learn, a new place to go, a novel thing to buy or do, an adventure or experience we've never had before, a gift we're about to open, or simply a brand new day. Any positive, affirming object or event we might see in our future and can look forward to will sustain our continuation as living beings, and keep us airborne or, if you wish, above ground in more ways than one.

The future, or our continuation as existing beings, is synonymous with what is just beyond the moment, like a new washing machine, an upcoming religious holiday, a birthday to celebrate, a new car to buy, a next-generation smartphone, or a brand-new film about to premiere.

Our future, our age, and the meaning of things

Another of the myriad ways The Structure and its mandate for continuation can be demonstrated is in the way older people often make a concerted effort to appear younger than they actually are. One's age, in most cultures, not only speaks to their past, but equally to their future as well. Youth is championed in some cultures with such intensity that many go to great expense to preserve a youthful appearance. Interestingly, the other extreme of time's relevancy is equally sought after. For example, which would you be most interested in holding in your hand, the oldest copy of the Bible or the newest? Or be most anxious to see, the first creature that ever lived or whatever is in existence now? Would you rather hug the oldest tree in the forest, or the newest sapling?

The age of things fascinates us because it underscores longevity, and something's longevity is proof positive that life can *con-*

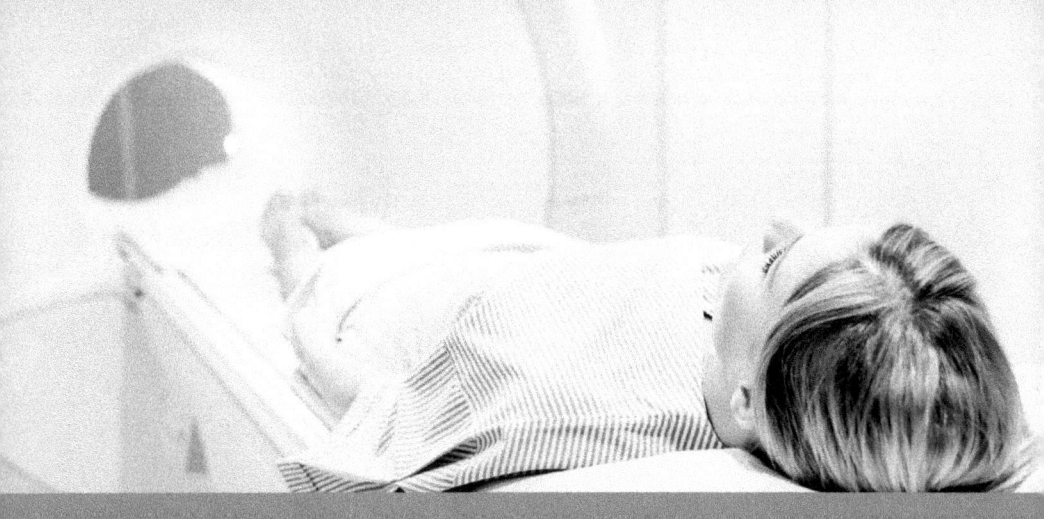

The Structure exercises the same influence over us regardless of changes to our physicality; our perceptions are what may change.

tinue on for a very long time, just like The Structure demands that it must.

Continuance and our experience of meaning

Understanding the etiology of meaning not only can help us understand what drives us to behave in certain ways but can edge us closer to understanding human conduct in general.

Things that last are things that mean something to us. When we find ourselves searching for an object or event's longevity, continuation, or temporal significance, we're actually searching for that object or event's meaning or value, a fact that also works the other way around.

A life-long friend, an eternal star, a continuously visited vacation spot, or even an everlasting fact or idea are meaningful when their images pass the test of time. If there is a strong signal of continuation, there will be a strong signal of meaning. "She

Continuance is simply our logical necessity to continue "being"; anything that is a signal to us that our lives will continue is affirming.

Death or **loss** are obvious examples of non-continuance; the extreme importance we give to our futures is also a way of understanding this imperative.

Ironically, the certainty of death gives life more meaning because of its immediate relationship to time.

means a lot to me. We've been friends forever," or "I've passed by that same veggie stand and waved to Mel every day now for 37 years." "Look through this and you see the most ancient star in our galaxy." There really are times when age can have a special sparkle—the sparkle of continuation that only yesterday's continuance into life's tomorrows can bring.

The meaning of life, the concept of value, and the role of death

Now that you know what the origin of meaning is, you're equipped to understand why many of us search for a meaning of life. This consideration brings us to the absence of continuation or, crudely put, **death**. Death is akin to an existential four-letter word as it points directly to a total collapse of The Structure. Death brings with it an end to all relational activity, an undoing of confirmation, and an across-the-board cessation of one's tomorrows. It means that something cannot continue being who or what it is, thereby blatantly violating each and every one of life's structural imperatives.

Curiously, death can also have a silver lining. (No joke!) Despite our innate resistance to it, knowing that there is a final chapter to life awakens us to appreciate life's value or meaning. Try, for example, to imagine that there were endless tomorrows. Would today have the same value or meaning for you as it does right now? When time limits are placed on certain events, the value of those events seem to automatically increase in unexpected ways. "Offered for a limited time only." "Time-sensitive material." "Only available this weekend." "Only once in every 10,000 years." "Macy's One-Day Sale." "One show only."

What we humans regard
as meaningful is ultimately
the result of an object's
or thought's supposed
temporal significance.

Age, at either end of one's life, is a common way that continuance manifests itself, as either the vigor of youth, or the regard paid to anyone who has reached an uncommonly old age.

Inside every
demand lies a
potential
contradiction.

CHAPTER 8

Demands and Expectations

We all have an aversion to being told what to do. But have you ever wondered why?

Behind every demand hides a contradiction. Unless we've voluntarily signed up for a specific demand scenario (like when we join a religious group, social club, or the military) demands or expectations are rarely welcomed.

Demands and relational polarity

All relational activity has a subject and an object. For example, if you have a relationship with your father, normally, you will be the subject of that relationship, and your father will be its object. If your father has a relationship with you, the same subject/object dynamic will take place, only in this case, your father will be the subject, with you taking on the role of the object. However, when your father expects or demands that you behave in a specific way, you've essentially been asked to become both the subject and the object of the same relationship at the same time which, of course, is impossible. As a result, being the logical entities that we are, when something is demanded of us, we first must correct any error in that demand's relational polarity; if we can't, we won't be able to complete the demand itself.

When, for example, we receive an unexpected, unsolicited, or random demand, The Structure will guide us to reset its (subject/object) polarity and place the relationship's polarity back where it belongs. Either that or refuse to be an accomplice in what would be the activation of a gross contradiction. To achieve this, the first thing The Structure will ask of us is to make sure that all implied parties of the demand are aware that a polarity correction has been made.

For example, someone who has been asked to do something might retort: "Do I have to!? Aw, come on, you gotta be kidding. You know I hate to do stuff like that." Either that, or the subject who received the demand will simply refuse to carry it out. For example, Nathan might demand that Susan do the dishes. But for Sue that would mean that she would no longer be the subject of doing the dishes, Nathan would! This structural anomaly would force Susan to refuse to comply with Nathan's demand. Either that, or Susan must make sure everyone who was privy to the demand know that she is not the subject of her actions; someone else is.

Another way to rectify a contradiction in relational polarity is to reclaim one's role as the subject. After all, it's only logical that we demand being the subject of our own lives. For example, you may hear someone say, "I know!" "I was already on my way!" or "That was the plan!"

Tell me what to do and I'll find a way around it

Melinda was making her weekly to-do list when her husband, Craig, walked in and told her to pick up his dry cleaning. "I've got a meeting with the boss tomorrow so don't forget my blue suit that's over at the High and

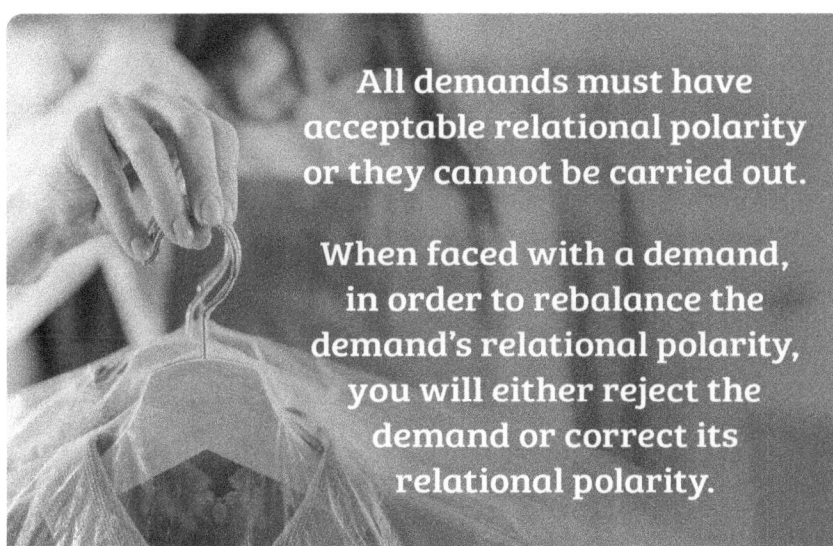

All demands must have acceptable relational polarity or they cannot be carried out.

When faced with a demand, in order to rebalance the demand's relational polarity, you will either reject the demand or correct its relational polarity.

Dry." Melinda felt her muscles go rigid. "I know, I know! It's already on my to-do list!" (Polarity reset.) When one announces their pre-knowledge of a potential demand, the relational polarity of the demand will remain in place. Under such conditions, for example Melinda will be allowed to remain the subject of her future action.

Melinda then walked upstairs and, passing her son Aaron's room, called out, "Wear your dark blue shirt. It's school picture day!"

Aaron had already laid out his dark blue shirt on his bed, but now, after his mom's bossy order, he couldn't bring himself to put it on. Instead, he went back to his closet and grabbed a different shirt. He had to. His mother just discombobulated the relational polarity her son had with his blue shirt, making it impossible for him to wear it. He could have replied, "I've already got it here on the bed!" but now it's too late for any polarity resetting, so he went to pick out a different shirt.

Arriving upstairs, Melinda peered in at her daughter Cleo and saw that Cleo was holding up two sweaters in front of the mirror trying to decide which one to wear. "Wear the pink one," her mother blurted out. "Got it!" And Cleo immediately put the pink sweater on—no problem! All her life, she and her mom had an unspoken agreement to help each other make fashion choices. With that voluntary relational setup between mother and daughter, all possible polarity problems are avoided, at least where fashion selections are concerned.

Demands and our relational Structure

Melinda fixed her relational polarity with Craig by insisting she already knew she had to pick up his suit. In doing so, she demonstrated that she was clearly the subject of the action she was about to engage in. As mentioned before, when someone demands or expects something from us, we often find ourselves either unable to complete the demand or in urgent need to clarify the relational polarity of the demand itself. In the same way, Aaron reclaimed the subject position by ignoring his mother's request and donning a different shirt. Problem solved!

Demand's power to manipulate value and the hidden power of obligation

Have you ever had a house guest who stayed way too long, and, with each passing day, made you feel more and more like a prisoner in your own home? But then, all of a sudden, they announce that they're leaving, and you find yourself once again appreciating your time with them.

Logic dictates that you be the subject of your life; demands coming from others often violate that logic.

You logically identify every action you engage in with who you are. You must always be the subject of your own life!

Demand and obligation can often affect how we value our relational environment; this is most obvious when we see how the lifting of an obligation can change one's behavior.

Why the change in how you valued your guest? The answer is simple. What had first been a case of misplaced polarity between you and your guest has now been suddenly reset, allowing your guest's value to return to what it was before they first arrived.

How about that incessantly bouncy cruise you took with the wife but finally ended (thankfully!)? Later, you got to thinking it wasn't so bad after all! Or that romantic partner that had gone stale, but when they announced that they were leaving you, your interest in them rekindled itself. Demands, in general, can be relationship killers. They can confuse relational polarity assignments and push subjects and objects out of relational kilter. When a demand is lifted, however, so will be its potentially contradicting nature, and the value of one's relational life will return to normal.

The presence of demand and the anxiety that frequently accompanies it, along with its yet unknown outcome, can twist and turn the value of people, events, and objects in the most unexpected of ways. Obligations can be double-edged swords and are often responsible for creating totally unforeseen emotions and behaviors. The next time you find that there's been a sudden shift in your perception of value, look a little closer. There's a good chance that some sort of demand was, from the beginning, behind it all.

When demands lose their punch

In cases in which one volunteers to be the object of a demand scenario, relational polarity is well established from the get-go, eliminating all contradictions that might be caused by polarity inversion. Like when someone joins the military or a religion, or takes on a membership in a fitness club or social group. Here, despite the sometimes-brutal nature of the demands being made, no contradictions of relational polarity will take place. Everyone will be aware of who the subject of those demands is and who is the object. The same holds true in the workplace. There will be no question who gets to make contradiction-free demands. That's the boss' job!

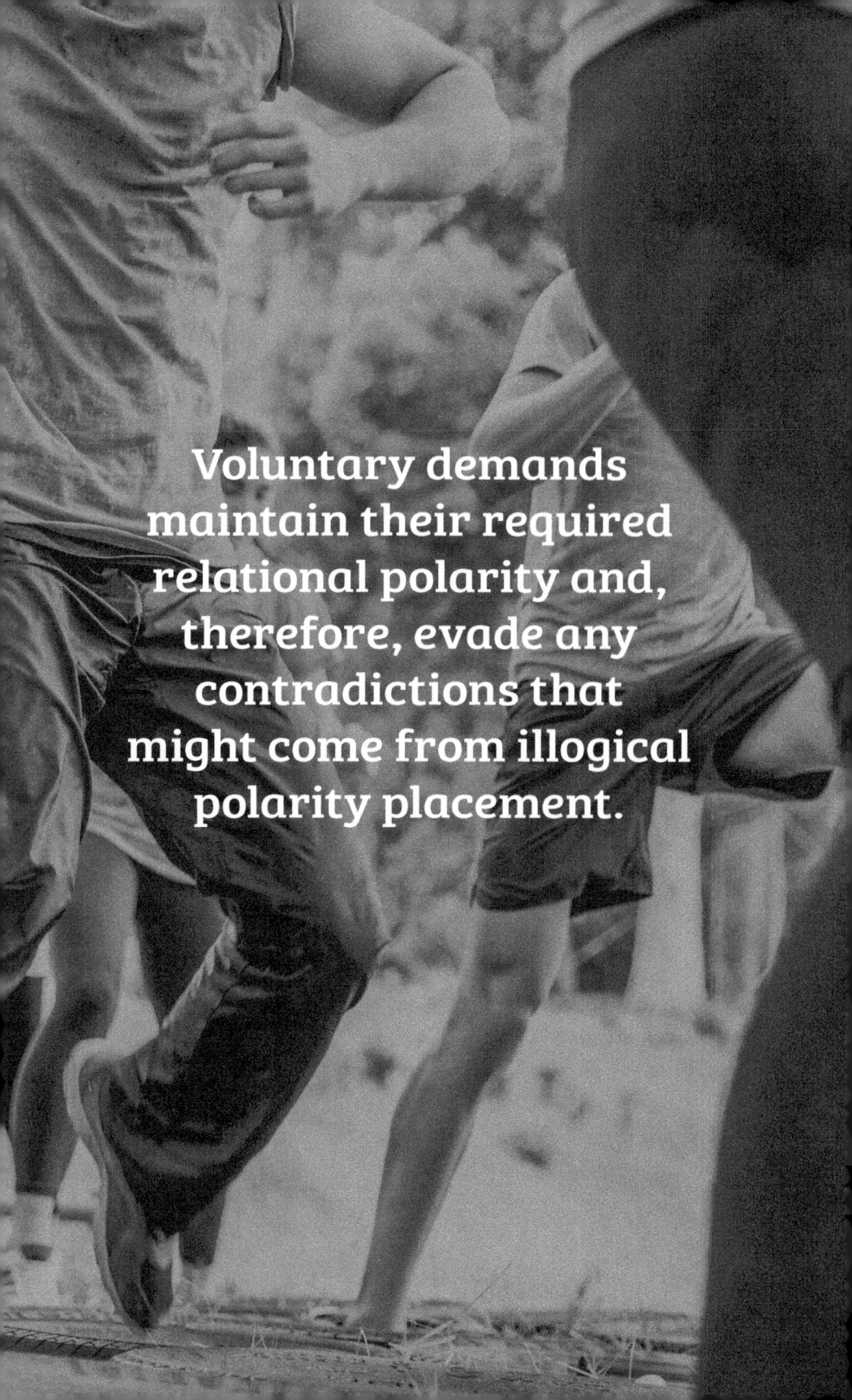

Voluntary demands maintain their required relational polarity and, therefore, evade any contradictions that might come from illogical polarity placement.

Who we are becoming is
always in flux,
as each environmental
confirmation takes part
in our ongoing evolution.

CHAPTER 9

Fitting Into Our Genes

From time to time, one might wonder why it is that some people behave in surprisingly similar ways when facing like circumstances, while others act so differently. Like when someone is anxiously waiting to parachute out of a plane, their heart racing and their palms sweating, yet the jumper next to them appears serene, or even joyful. What makes these two people feel and behave so differently when facing precisely the same situation?

Most of us experience our world in vastly different ways. This is due to the vastly different interplay that can exist between each one of our individual DNA codes and each one of our individually unique relational environments. No one is genetically the same as another, nor is able to experience the world around them in exactly the same way. As a matter of fact, you and I can be standing before the same exact work of art and see quite different things. It's a question of each one of our individual physically and psychologically generated perspectives that make the difference.

Nurture or nature?

Which is it? What leans heaviest on the way we think, feel, and behave? Is it who we are genetically or who we're constantly becoming through our environmental experiences?

It's both!

The first thing you should keep in mind about the way we are structured is that, like a coin that can't be what it is without the

presence of both of its sides, we can't exist without the two sides that make us who we are: our genetic side or genetic selves, and our ever-changing environmental selves. As said before, there is nothing new about the idea that our environment has an impact on our behavior. For decades researchers have surmised that who we are genetically, along with the environments we live in, form the active ingredients that make up our individual personalities and, of course, how we ultimately behave. What has been hidden from us until now is the role each one of these causal elements plays in the behavior they create.

The Structure's building blocks

Each one of us is born with our own personal, concrete genetic traits and tendencies, or if you wish, entirely unmatched genetic selves. Our DNA is what helps make us the individuals we are. It affects our height, our facial features, the color of our skin, the way we walk, and the tenor of our voice. It determines how we express ourselves, gesture, and prefer one color or kind of food over another. But the power of who we are genetically

> **Our genetic and environmental selves form an inseparable bond; our two selves, forever intertwined to make one *self*, define who we are and who we are forever becoming.**

doesn't stop there. Our genes also regulate the way we perceive the world around us, how we shape our ideas, and how we react emotionally to this stimulus or that. More importantly still, our genes give us the personalities that will remain with us for the rest of our lives.

Our genetic selves, however, can no more exist all by themselves than can that coin we mentioned exist without its other side. If a gene hasn't an environment to relate to, it's just a useless piece of genetic material about to disappear entirely.

None of us can exist until our genetic selves are united with their relational counterparts or environments. That's how you, I, and every other living thing on this planet are put together. We are the union of our genetic selves as they relate to the world around them. Simply put, every living thing is a relational phenomenon. That's the way we are physically and psychologically structured, and the fundamental reason why the object world around us feels as vitally important to us as it does. Truth be told, *we can't live without it!*

Our behavior changes as our cumulative experiences reveal better ways of achieving our goals; life can be easier if we learn that lesson well.

And life marches on!

Our relational environment is in constant flux and, therefore, so are we. Because other things and other people can be as affirming as they can be contradicting, so can we. Given that there is a dynamic that exists between our genetic selves and our ever-changing environmental selves, one could say that all living things are works in perpetual progress.

Like our smartphones that are continually updating themselves, we, too, are continually updating who we are. This we do by engaging with the ever-changing relational environment that envelops us. We learn that we can acquire certain goals using this tactic or that, prevent certain contradictions by employing one method or the other. A toddler who screams because they want their mother to buy them a toy, but receives nothing for their efforts, soon learns that such behavior doesn't get them what they want, so they stop behaving that way. Strong, self-sacrificing mothers and fathers have a better chance of producing ordered upbringings for their children, that is if they can stand being psychologically waterboarded for a while before they see any real results.

The fellow who can never get a date hopefully may someday realize that if he at least took a shower every once in a while and brushed his hair, life might go a whole lot better for him. In both these mundane examples, nobody changes their DNA nor their environment. They simply learn that by modifying certain facets of their behavior, they'll have a better chance of reaching their needs and goals. Simply put, and as if you already didn't know it, by applying lessons learned through the experiences we have, life can sometimes go easier on us.

The home guard

Ever since she was born, Silvia had maintained a positive relationship with her parents. For years they'd been her primary relational support system. Her mom and dad had constantly been there for her, supporting her in every way. That's why she becomes as emotionally affected as she does when they criticize her, and lately they've been doing a lot of that. She'd always shied away from rebuking their criticisms for fear of getting on their wrong side, yet more and more she's felt a need to do something definitive about the negative relational confirmations she'd been receiving from them lately.

So-called "inner conflicts"

In classical psychology, what Silvia suffers from is commonly referred to as an inner conflict. But what are inner conflicts in reality, and what causes them? During the past two centuries, psychologists have referred to psychological events like these as being interior to the human psyche. But then again, is there a psychological event that isn't?

With our new understanding of how we are psychologically designed, we now know that so-called inner conflicts are simply conflicts that take place between our genetic selves and our environmental selves, and are no more or no less interior to us than any other brand of conflictive relational activity. In Silvia's case, a conflict occurs when her genetic self is contradicted by the relationship she has with her loving parents, an occurrence that invariably causes a difficult-to-resolve dilemma. How can Silvia satisfy her need to neutralize the contradictions she is receiving from her parents when what she needs to neutralize is such a large part of who she is? (We are our environment.) That's a good question and speaks to a psychological occurrence that is as pervasive as the common cold.

Normally, this type of conflict can be resolved through dialogue or simple communication between the involved parties. Other times, however, if a mutual resolution cannot be found, the original source of the conflict may be associated with contradiction itself and, therefore, relationally distanced from the person who feels contradicted. Like when a parent quite purposely distances themselves from a contradicting child, a good friend suddenly becomes one's worst enemy, a loved one

Classical psychology uses the term "inner conflicts" to describe a structural dynamic where one's genetic self is at odds with its environmental self, a contradictory scenario that is all too common.

is suddenly and for no apparent reason left by the wayside, or a once-revered job suddenly feels more like a punishment.

More on inner conflict

As you must have noticed, there are any number of psychological behaviors that the union between who we are genetically and our relational environment create. When our two selves (genetic and environmental) coincide in their needs and goals, our identities are easily affirmed by those around us, and our lives feel that they are on solid footing. For example, if we're born with an affinity to read, and we live surrounded by avid readers, we're golden. But many times environments are not at all in sync with one's genetically spawned talents or desires, and they find that their two selves are working against each other.

Forced to operate in conflict mode, inner conflicts can quickly arise, causing emotional responses that heavily influence the way we behave. Understanding this, it's easy to see how daily life can inflict multiple jabs to our emotional health. Often these are simple, mundane prods, like wanting an ice cream cone but finding the ice cream shop closed, or needing silence when someone's car alarm won't stop blaring. But other times, contradictions of this nature can take on more sinister tones.

When we say that our genetic selves can come into conflict with our environmental selves, remember that, just like that two-sided coin that desperately needs its both sides to be what it is, the only way we can be who we are is by having our genetic selves bound, like conjoined twins, to our environment. After all, cementing ourselves to our environment is the only way we can "be" in the first place, and yet for many of us, that structural obligation can already spell divergence, conflict, and subsequent misery.

Another inner conflict case in point

When we are genetically driven to love classical music, but born into a culture that abhors the classics, conflict will arise because our most immediate environment inherently contradicts who we are. Or, we have no interest in sports, yet form a part of a sports-loving family. In both cases our genetic self will immediately be at odds with our environmental self and doomed to experience instant contradiction.

Since who we are is genetically bound to our environmental selves (i.e., the rules, values, and general whims of our society), one vital portion of who we are can't live without the other.

This structurally required union between genetics and environment, nature and nurture can become, with nobody even half trying, a powder keg of discrepancy.

Home sweet home

After walking through the front door, Sarah made a bee-line for her bedroom sanctuary. It's where she spent most of her time these days. It was where she felt safe, locked away from criticism and misunderstanding. She knew that her parents meant well and probably loved her. Still, it didn't feel right being around them lately. Clearly, they were disappointed with the choices she'd been making. That, and her lackluster performance.

Sarah knew that she was nothing like Marcus, her superstar brother, and obviously the favorite of the family. Even young Andy seemed to please their parents most of the time, as he tried hard to be like Marcus. But not Sarah. Sarah was never good enough.

"Time for dinner," her mother yelled up the stairs. Attendance was mandatory, so Sarah made her way to the table to endure another round of "Let's Compare the Kids," knowing she'll come in last...again. At least this time around it was pizza night, a small consolation that made Fridays only slightly more bearable than usual. They all slide into their assigned seats, and the games began.

"How was school today?" kicked off round one in a predictable way. Sarah felt the dread rise from her stomach and stick inside her throat like a rubber ball. It was the same thing every night. The same questions. The same answers. The same disapproval masked by forced smiles. The same arrogant, amused looks on her perfect brothers' faces.

"Epic!" Marcus always answered first. "I aced my calc exam, and Coach told me I am definitely starting quarterback this year. I totally knew it!" he announced with a level of confidence boarding on cocky. It was obvious that the parents ate up every word.

Dad, beaming at his oldest son, gives him the typical "Atta boy. You always make us so proud. Can't wait 'til the season starts—we'll be at every game. Right, guys?" he asks nobody in particular, which clearly meant everybody.

Sarah resisted a roll of the eyes with such ferocity that her left cheek started twitching. But knowing she was in a dismal minority, kept her displeasure to herself. Why provoke her dad? He'd just give that same tired speech about not understanding why she didn't want to "show up for this family." So she kept her eyes still while she stuffed her feelings down past that rubber ball that was still uncomfortably lodged in her throat. If she zoned out a little at least she wouldn't cry. That always made everything even more awkward. How dare she remind everyone that she not only sucked at sports and lived for art class, but that she was "so sensitive," as if that were some kind of disease! Why couldn't she just accept her lot? Life was hard enough. Why was she making hers so much harder than it needed to be? Why couldn't she just try to fit in? Her brothers were both so good at it.

Our example, in review

The example above shows us how when someone's genetically anchored personality coincides with the values, needs, and goals of the rest of his or her relational environment, one could say that a minor miracle has taken place. But this, of course, isn't the way life usually plays out. There are endless, unpredictable genetic combinations out there, and an infinite variety of possible relational environments, all providing far too many opportunities for parallel instead of coincidental existences to be found in intimate proximity. Don't get me wrong. Perfect genetic/environmental scenarios can and do take place, but then again, so do blue moons.

It is far more common that, like Sarah, some people simply don't fit in with the expectations and values of those who form their most immediate social milieu. Maybe this is the situation you once were subjected to, or are being subjected to right now. If that's the case, don't be surprised by the emotional state you find yourself in. Just know that you are not alone. Being out of sync with one's environment is the gold standard of our psychological lives and responsible for the lion's share of our emotional conundrums.

Obviously, even though getting along or fitting in are excellent ways to avoid contradiction, it can be a real challenge to be someone you're not! As a matter of fact, it can't be done. We can, however, change our behavior, although, that can only happen when we do so on our own terms.

Changing our behavior can invite more contradiction

As discussed before, desperate situations sometimes require desperate solutions. Even though this is true sometimes, when our lives become too conflictive for us, we can be, at times, forced into changing our behavior in the hope that we will finally receive some affirming echo from our environment. Doing so, unfortunately, can be a catalyst for conflict. When, for example, we've artificially changed our behavior and now are receiving positive feedback, there is a good chance that we will not feel deserving of that feedback. After all, in reality, the affirmations we're receiving are not really directed at us at all, but rather at a fabricated role we're playing. Consequentially, our selves become self-contradicting, and instead of solving an urgent problem, we've just created another.

No matter what, in Sarah's case it would be practically impossible for her to carry out such a ruse as the divide that exists between who she is and what her relational environment demands she be is too great. She could try pretending as if she cared about football or sports in general, but that's not what she was being asked to do. She was being asked to stop being Sarah and, instead, be someone who is studious, energetic, and

When who we are coincides with the norms
of our environment, it's smooth sailing.
When there is little agreement,
life's waters invariably get rough.

emotionally impenetrable while, all at the same time, loving and compliant with those demands that constantly come from the family HQ.

Can changing your environment alleviate psychological discord?

Yes, it can. If you detect that your relational environment is causing you insurmountable amounts of displeasure and pain, you have the option of simply moving on. Many of us do. Changing our relational environment to coincide with our needs and goals is a common solution to the psychological stress created by our often non-coinciding genetic selves.

For example, at 18 years of age, many young adults exit the family unit and can be, consequentially, relieved from the psychological strain they had been living under. Those who are unhappy at their jobs seek new ones. If a child is ridiculed at school for being nerdish, switching to a school that reveres the talents many so-called nerdish folk have can be life-changing. If there's too much conflictive discourse at home, one might find themselves going for frequent long walks, moving to the basement, or simply getting out of Dodge entirely. Remember, there's a reason why others are asking you to change. "You" form an integral part of who they are as well, yet your way of being is in contradiction with their structurally built mold. Your presence among them can be as contradictory for them as they can be for you.

Relief is possible, temporarily

When it comes to our genetic/environmental lot in life, good or bad luck can change our situation from being hostile to being welcoming or, of course, the other way around. Such fortuitous changes in our lives can even make us feel as though we, too, have changed. But we haven't. It's only our circumstances that have. Fortunately, or unfortunately, events like this are usually fleeting. Think back to Emily and her lucky jackpot. There was nothing about who she was that created her post-windfall life condition. It wasn't Emily that had changed, it was only Emily's environmental circumstances that had. Emily was a hard-working gal who'd been left on the side of life's road to fend for herself. Then, all of a sudden, that lucky scratcher brought her (as it would have brought most of us), some welcomed, albeit temporary relief from her psychological misfortunes. But again, most of the time, any relief that one's good fortune may bring will have an expiration date, after which life will snap back to its old self.

As mentioned before, each one of our genetic selves is unchangeable, so how nice it is when, because of an uncooperative environment, we have access to a good therapist, religious guide, counselor, best friend, or willing-to-listen bartender—someone who will replace a contradicting relational environment with an affirming one.

Are there any other tools out there we can use to find relief from contradiction?

Of course, there are! Something else that can help us get from one day to the next is simply understanding why we are feeling the way we are. Understanding what makes us tick is a masterful contradiction canceler. You should try it! Knowledge and understanding can go the distance when it comes to battling contradiction and the loss of control we often feel when conflict takes over our lives.

Self-esteem, and those big, golden plastic trophies

Ever wondered what all the fuss is about our current self-esteem crisis? It seems like a fad that just won't go away. Youngsters everywhere—and not just those who suffer from a poor self-image—are showered with unwarranted symbols of success. It seems that someone out there thought that being positive and ever-encouraging to others, especially younger folks, would cure us of our self-image glitches. As a result, during these last three or so decades, youngsters living in developed countries

Undeserved affirmation intended to bolster self-esteem can lead to harder contradictions down the road.

have been given unearned congratulations and undeserved prizes for uninspiring behavior. This, with the idea that such will automatically lift everyone's self-image and make the world a better place.

Parents are prompted to do the same at home, and compliment their child for the slightest accomplishment, like getting on a swing without falling, exiting their bed on time, eating all their cereal, or brushing their teeth at night.

In addition, psychologists have, over the decades, instructed parents, counselors, and school staffers to do whatever they can to convince their charges that they are special, unique, or exceptional, even when, clearly, they are none of the above.

Artificial, unwarranted signs of esteem and admiration coming from one's relational environment are a frequently used tactic intended to solve a problem that cannot be solved through false or artificial means. Indeed, inauthentic relational feedback can, eventually, be far more harmful to young people than allowing them to confront the reality of life's frequently contradictory ways.

Keep in mind that anyone who has been living under false pretexts will naturally be unprepared to deal with real-world conflict and, therefore, far more likely to succumb to the pressures of reality than someone who has been dealing with contradiction from the get-go. Conflicts accompanied by support and understanding prepare us for the future. Granted, learning can often be painful, but pain experienced now and in ways that are properly managed can mean less pain later and far more understanding. In a word, perhaps keeping it real is not such a bad idea after all.

The long arm of the environment

As we've just explored, the influence that our environment has over us is remarkable. It forms an indispensable part of who we are and, as such, wields an enormous amount of power over the way we direct our lives.

Treading in deep waters

"You're the man, George!" Being on the shy side, George wasn't used to getting so much attention, but his friends loved the idea of personally knowing a potential hero. And if George was honest with himself, he loved the positive relational echo he'd been getting from doing the things he did. His best friend Emilio was always the loudest voice in George's makeshift fan club. "Why don't

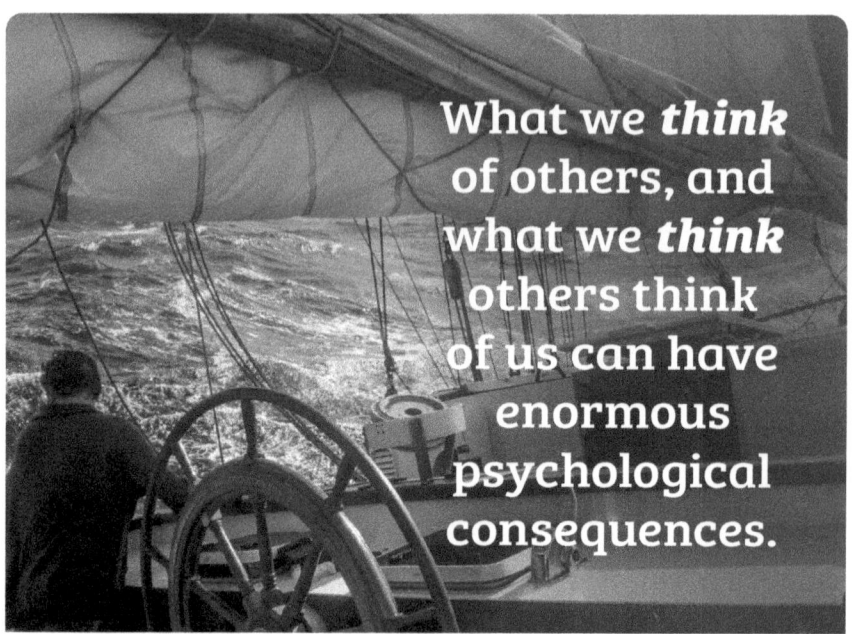

What we *think* of others, and what we *think* others think of us can have enormous psychological consequences.

you go big? You're ready, right? Take on the whole damn Atlantic. Your mom and dad will be in the Canaries this summer so you could make that your first stop, then go the rest of the way to Málaga, no?"

George loved to sail. It was his passion. But he typically took care to make decisions based on trustworthy data and evidence, always erring on the side of reason; resisting the urge to let his passion override his judgment. He had made a number of journeys along America's Eastern Seaboard, each time building confidence, each time going a little farther. But now, everyone seemed to be talking about crossing the entire Atlantic Ocean!

Meantime, the praise and admiration kept flowing George's way. His genetically inspired cautious side was trying to talk some sense into his environmental side but all the affirmation he was being given ultimately won out, and George decided to make the crossing. His parents were, quite naturally, apprehensive, especially George's mom. They had tried, again and again to have George rethink his plans, but as the days and weeks passed, George became more and more convinced that he should sail off as his environment expected him to.

And yet, this only half-seasoned sailor also had his doubts, and they were serious ones. It was risky out there, and yet the environmental pressures kept building, then building some more. There were now thousands who were cheering George on. Then, several days before the voyage George consulted NOAA and discovered that there was a severe storm brewing off the southwest Caribbean that could directly threaten his plans. Rogue waves were not uncommon in the part of the Atlantic he would be traveling over, and he knew that just one of those could sink his boat in a heartbeat.

Several days before the voyage George slept badly. He'd consulted those predictions over and over hoping there'd be a change, but everything remained the same.

George's parents called everyone they knew to try and convince their son that he should wait for the following spring; better yet, not go at all. But that changed nothing. The departure day arrived, and it seemed that the whole world was present for the grand send-off. Deep down George felt that he was making a serious mistake, but knew that if he called the whole thing off now he'd look like a wimp, a wimp with a capital W.

Television cameras from the local news station had been set up on the jetty, and he was encouraged to give interviews to the press. It was a beautiful sunny day, but George knew what was waiting for him just beyond all those beautiful, fair-weather clouds. At the same time, powerful environmental contradictions were waiting for him were he to suddenly change his mind and stay home. As a result, among cheers and waving fans, George set sail.

Six days later radio contact with his boat was lost, and by the month's end, George had been declared lost at sea.

Why we take risks

George's genetic self knew better, but the environmental influences he received won out in the end. Are such scenarios predictable? Yes, they certainly are. Realize, for example, that whenever we feel more familiar with *now* than we do about *later*, it will usually be now that we go with.

George, for example, knew all about his "now" and it was tangibly filled with limelight, expectation, and basket-loads of positive confirmation. "Later" remained an enigma, but now was a no brainer. As a result, George went with now. After all, now George was receiving the almost magical positive power provided by what he *thought* others were thinking about him.

What we *think* of others and what we *think* others think of us contains enormous psychological significance and will often compel us to follow society's ways of affirming others. Remember, even though The Structure is systematized logically, human behavior is under no particular mandate to behave in clearly-defined, logical ways.

Magical thinking

Back in the early 1900s Swiss psychologist Jean Piaget observed that human thought could feel "magical"; a belief that many of us still hold as true today. In other words, that our thoughts have special powers, like the ability to make things appear and disappear, change the course of time, modify the future, or even moderate human life entirely. But can they?

Expressions like "Think like that and you'll have him turning in his grave." "Be careful what you wish for." "We're *thinking* of you." Or, "I *thought* that would happen," we all take seriously. But why?

As we now know, there is a pivotal relationship between who we are and the relational confirmations we receive from our environment. We also know that we humans are the most expressive of all beings. Consequentially, it's only logical to assume that the confirmations that indicate to us who and what we are, must come from what we think others think of us. If we assume that others think positively of us, our lives can move happily along. However, when we think that they don't, our days can darken.

Many of us are subconsciously aware of the psychological power others have over us and feel that we are victims of that power. Consequently, many of us fight tooth and nail to convince ourselves that we can psychologically survive divorced from those around us. And yet, we secretly know that such beliefs are more the product of wishful thinking than anything else.

In reality, without the virtual or concrete confirmations we receive, or *think* we receive, from animate or inanimate things, our lives could not continue. If, for example, you *think* that someone, or a group of people, believe you to be a slacker, good-looking, inept, a genius, stupid, superbly talented, or a master of wit, such feelings will unquestionably affect you. They can comfort or depress you, bring you joy or despair, make your day or ruin it completely.

Human thoughts, human beliefs

Human thought may not be magical, but it definitely is a powerful psychological phenomenon. That's why we hang on as tightly as we do to our core beliefs, even when the facts may not validate them. We have the impression that, were we to abandon those beliefs, we would abandon our very selves. Remember, our beliefs come from without, not from within, yet they are a primary source of our emotional strength. It should come as no surprise, therefore, that whatever we *think, suppose, guess,* or *assume* others think of us can wield immense power over our psychological well-being. In fact, what we *think* others think of us will always affect us psychologically.

That's why we will often take care not to *think* badly of someone we love or admire, as though it might actually hurt them. Or if we hope for something, we'll knock on wood in order to keep our wishes from backfiring. Telling a friend that we'll be *thinking* about them lends special importance to the relationship we have with that person, and by placing a monument in the village square, we're convinced that its presence will keep others *thinking* about the individual depicted and, somehow, even return a smattering of life to them.

Understanding that human thought is a prime mover of our emotions is not as crazy as it might seem as it's supported by structural fact. One just shouldn't take this kind of phenomena too far out of the purely psychological domain where it exclusively belongs.

Cultural clashes

Viraj was always embarrassed to go out with his mother. In fact, he wished he could just pretend he wasn't related to anyone in his family at all! If only he could just have a normal name and live a normal life! He was American, after all. Born in Chicago, he spoke with an intentionally heavy American accent, and he tried his best to melt into his surroundings. He so wanted to be just another member of all things red, white, and blue. Why couldn't his parents act like everybody else? Why did they have to wear those outfits? It's humiliating! Why in the world did his mother have to wear saris in public? American women don't wear saris, only women who lived in India did. America wasn't India. It was America!

"I do not like the way you disrespect your mother, Viraj," his father would chide. Viraj's behavior had been reprimanded over and over. "You go to your room. You will not be coming with us on our outing today."

"Great! I don't want to be seen in public with you like that anyway. Why can't you just dress like everybody else?"

"I do dress like everyone else where we come from," his mother would insist. "It is our custom. I am still the same person I was in India. I will not change who I am to please you or the other people in this country. I am proud of my culture. And, by the way, it's your culture too. I hope that one day you will come to understand that."

As Viraj made his way to his room he mumbled under his breath, "Good luck with that! That's never going to happen. That's not me!" Viraj had never even been to India. The boy had nothing to do with India, and yet, had everything to do with America.

Because we are our environment

As we've reviewed several times, *Structured Psychology's* approach to human behavior demonstrates that the only way any living thing can continue existing is by constantly relating to its environment. In other words, either our genetic selves maintain themselves in relationship with the world around them, or we simply cannot continue being. As a result, no one can separate their relational environment from who they are genetically. It's simply not possible.

How do these facts relate to Viraj? Viraj is his genetically born self *plus* everything he's ever experienced: like his home, his parents, his school, and his friends, all of which are contained in the central American city of Chicago, but not in Delhi or Mumbai. He'd never even been to India. He had nothing to do with that distant nation; the psychological bond he had with his parents was with them, but not with their birth nation and only very distantly, with that birth nation's culture.

The Structure and cultural conflict

According to the way we are structured, our self-image has no choice other than to come from our relational environment.

It is thanks to how the needs of our genetic selves stack up against the values of that environment that we will have, at least, some sort of idea who we might be. Relationships between our genetic selves and our environmental selves form our total self. Equally, in order for the self to be psychologically affected, it must maintain a constant relationship with that portion of its outside world that affects it. Viraj felt nothing for his parents' homeland for the simple reason that he'd never had a concrete relationship with the environment in which they both had been brought up. It's hard to get all worked up over something you've never experienced.

The Structure and the birth of racism

A very similar relational dynamic plays out in the creation of racist thinking. When we find ourselves hard-pressed to accept certain unfamiliar cultures or people, values, or behaviors, we can easily be categorized as racist (one of humankind's most common psycho-social ailments). Exclusively because of the way we're structured, a person or culture that doesn't coincide with who we are has the logical tendency to be experienced as contradicting. Many contrasting experiences do.

It's no wonder that many of us have the tendency to reject contradictions generated by the difference between relating subjects and objects. Differences in opinion, values, and beliefs put us on the defensive because they threaten and, therefore, contradict our selves; selves that are, in part, the direct product of the relational echoes we receive from the society to which we are structurally beholden. People and things that are familiar to us affirm who we are, while unfamiliar things and people have

Any person or culture that doesn't coincide with who we are has the logical tendency to be experienced as contradicting.

the potential of doing just the opposite. It's not a steadfast rule that all things that contrast with who we are be experienced as contradictory, but it should be no surprise when they do.

Take someone who is brought up in an area where most public buildings are covered by graffiti. They will feel perfectly at home in such surroundings, whereas those who rarely see graffiti might feel threatened or out of place when surrounded by publicly painted walls, store fronts, bridges, and so on. People who have lived for extended periods of time in social milieus where most have dark skin will naturally feel comforted by the presence of other dark-skinned people yet may feel ill at ease in places where most people have lighter skin tones. Being forced to remain in a contradicting social environment can cause distress, fearfulness, and anxiety because it's structurally illogical to have part of ourselves identified with something that we are not.

What determines structural virtuality?
What determines structural reality?

From a strictly psychological perspective, the only way a relational experience can be considered real is determined by one's level of *conviction* that it is. Adam may refuse to watch the day's news if it's been announced that they will be showing soldiers being shot to death. The reality of the video might deal him a contradiction he couldn't easily neutralize. However, after being convinced by a conspiracy theorist that the two planes that crashed into the Twin Towers were just holograms, Adam has no emotional problem watching over and over again those clips of that attack on the United States.

Keeping our relational environments virtual

In order to avoid being hurt by our own actions, many of us prefer to keep some of our relationships strictly on a virtual level. For example, when we look away from a road accident, our intention is to avoid being affected emotionally by what we might see, or cover our ears if we suspect that we may hear something that might be difficult to neutralize. Seeing something with our own eyes or hearing something directly from the horse's mouth, as it were, helps convince us that what we are experiencing is real, not virtual.

For similar reasons, deceased people are put under a sheet. Among other reasons, placing a sheet over them places that person's death in a virtual sphere. Out of sight; out of mind. If we actually see the deceased, the contradictory nature of their lifeless body will, in part, become ours, and we already know how contradicting death can be to life. This is just one example of how the psychological impact of certain relationships can be offset by virtuality: hide it, cover it, sweep it under the rug, close the door behind it, or just forget that thing or event ever happened.

Our virtual lives: cell phones, video games, and social media

Looking away from an accident or placing a sheet over someone who is deceased are just two mundane examples of how we sometimes regulate the potentially damaging effects of convincing contradiction. Keeping certain experiences as not at all persuasive or only virtual helps fend off contradiction, at least the kind we feel we must neutralize. We might, for example, cover our ears and make extraneous noises to avoid hearing what we suspect would be best left on a virtual plane. Leaving the room when we know that someone is about to recount an upsetting experience will save us from the story's full relational impact. Calling someone on the phone instead of seeing them in person can attenuate the potentially damaging power of a possible contradiction that a face-to-face encounter might produce. Texting someone might be a better option still if what one desires is immunity from a possible direct, difficult-to-neutralize contradiction.

A platonic romance for someone might be more palatable than the real thing. Playing a video game where imaginary but violent figures are involved in despicable actions keeps its players from suddenly coming down with a severe case of PTSD. And watching the already-played highlights of a crucial tennis match on the internet may prove more agreeable, for some, than nervously watching the actual match as it unfolds in real time.

The flip side of the virtual relationship

In the reverse scenario of The Structure's relational equation, if our expectation is to enjoy something enriching, positive or forward-gazing, many of us will prefer to do so in person and, thereby, in a way that better *convinces* us that we are involved in a real relationship, and not one that is shielded by virtuality. For example, instead of speaking to a guru via Zoom we might prefer to physically be in his or her actual presence. Most would choose to be physically with their sweetheart instead of just talking to them on FaceTime. Listening to Brahms on a home sound system might bring us joy, but not half as much as if we're able to listen to the same concert live in a music hall. Many prefer sitting in the stands cheering at the playoffs in lieu of watching them on TV. And viewing stars through a telescope can be more engaging than seeing them painted on the ceiling of a planetarium.

There are countless examples of how we're able reap the benefits of actual, convincingly real experiences over those that convince us not at all of their authenticity.

In other examples, instead of just lamenting the death of a loved one, we might personally place flowers on their grave, or instead of sending a last-minute Christmas email to a good friend, we might spend the time and effort to send them an actual hand-written card through the mail. Personally serving the food at a shelter during Thanksgiving may be far more emotionally fulfilling, for some, than just making a donation to the Salvation Army.

Delineating a protective space around our relational interactions by making them virtual may reduce or even eliminate possible contractions, while those we hope to derive pleasurable confirmations from are best experienced in person or in a convincingly real setting. The list of how we are able to manipulate the psychological impact of relationships by manipulating their virtual/non-virtual nature is extensive. Keep your eyes open and you'll begin to notice just how common they are.

Luddites, tech junkies, and the Industrial Revolution
At this point I should mention the palatable differences that exist between many of the relational situations we are exposed to today compared to those we were confronted with only a few decades ago. Today, we can often obtain things we feel we might need to overcome life's smaller, mundane challenges, and do it in a heartbeat. Here I'm referring to this work-reducing, gadget-minded society we've created for ourselves, and how commerce has found a way to line its pockets as it satisfies our desire to try and defend ourselves from that great big contradiction-filled world out there.

Toward the end of the 1700s, thanks to the Industrial Revolution and its socio-commercial transformation, new machines and devices began to appear on the scene that promised to alleviate some of the common contradictions most of us had been subjected to up until that time. Devices that would lift us from floor to floor, wash our clothes for us, weave yarn into fabric, remove dirt from the floor, heat our homes, move us effortlessly from place to place, or blow one's hair dry at the push of a button.

The inventions that blossomed during that time (and continue to do so) proved themselves to be effective contradiction combatants, and have, ever since, seen their popularity skyrocket. As the years and decades have gone by, all manner of transportation systems have begun moving people and goods faster, easier, and over longer distances, allowing industry's goals to be reached quicker and more painlessly than the time before.

With the advent of the Industrial Revolution, we began feeling more and more in control of our lives, and more and more capable of fending off its more common contradictions. But that was just the beginning. Today, tech giants make us wonder how life could have ever been lived without our color TVs, smartphones, ultra-fast computers, and self-driving cars!

Then again, you may wonder: Is it possible that any of these clever contradiction tamers might have a downside?

Don't get me started!

The two faces of high-technology

Quite contrary to what one might think, due to our increased communication resources, the number of contradictory relationships we are exposed to has easily kept pace with all the new contradictions that before had been kept from us. Just a short time ago, the total amount of negative news we had access to came primarily from our daily lives, local newspaper, and maybe a weekly magazine. Today we're inundated with unforgiving tidal waves of shocking information that is no farther away from us than our shirt pockets, car radios, or handbags. As should be expected, the psychological consequences of being exposed to such gargantuan amounts of negative relational confirmation has an equally negative impact on how we feel psychologically. Why is there such a plethora of easily accessed negative information instead of information that encourages or promotes healthy relational activity? As usual, good news is hard to peddle, while bad news sells like hot cakes.

The structural nature of the news

Humans have always been drawn to the news, no matter where it came from. This is because the news has a surprising amount to do with The Structure's imperative of *continuation*.

Bad news, in particular, has additional appeal. It's invariably someone else's bad news, not our own, and that's important. Hearing that lung cancer is on the rise, or a train just derailed, killing hundreds in a country whose name we can't pronounce, has a very different impact on us than hearing that a loved one has been struck with a hard-to-cure disease or just perished in an air crash. But why? Why is it that we're anxious to hear of someone else's unsuccessful confrontation with contradiction but, in most cases, would just as well skip learning of any contradictions that affect us personally? For many, it's just common sense. Bad news that concerns someone else shines a brighter light on how fortunate we are as it relativizes, in our favor, whatever contradictions we might be facing at the time.

There is yet another psychological factor that makes someone else's contradictions appealing to others. Remember the expression, "Misery loves company?" There's a reason for that phenomenon, and the reason is structural. As it turns out, since each one of us identifies ourselves with our environment, we sense that what happens to us should logically be shared by anyone else that occupies our relational space. When it doesn't, we feel emotionally shortchanged. It's just not logical to feel singled out in a world in which we form an intimate structural

Modern communications and massive media coverage of life's events have a decisive impact on many of the relational confirmations we receive.

bond to be the only one suffering the pain of contradiction. We know that our lives depend on others but that reality should be mutually experienced just like The Structure dictates that it should.

Technology's upside: quick and easy affirmation

Is there an upside to today's technological advances? Yes, of course there is. Being able to instantly communicate with friends and family has made it easier to keep relationships more active, closer, and numerous. Opinion polls have the potential of becoming more accurate. Instant information can save lives by quickly locating people who are in distress. Clerical work can be accomplished in half the time. Propulsion mechanisms run better and far more efficiently. The information industry in general can now reach millions instead of just thousands. And the list goes on.

Unfortunately, while today's brand of technology clearly has its upsides, it's now become far too easy for many of us to fall into endless scrolling patterns on our phones or computers, thereby reducing our face-to-face relational activity to life-suffocating levels of virtuality. Now, because we have the option of risking less and less of ourselves as we virtually relate to others, that's often what we choose to do. Keeping ourselves at significant distances from concrete relational activity may keep us safe from real contradiction, but consequentially, it also keeps us from accessing the kind of solid, maturity-building relational action The Structure would prefer we had. The more we live lives of passive experiences, the less contact we will have with true affirmations and real contradictions, and the less prepared we will be to deal with the real world.

Relational debt and everyday life

Have you ever questioned why some of us feel the need to pay back something to our communities? For example, by participating in community-oriented activities, like serving meals at a soup kitchen, helping to clean local streets or parks, working at a voting booth, or helping out at a donation center. This is no vague construct. In many over-developed nations, thanks to a heightened use of virtual living, citizens have become so separated from their individual communities that they're no longer aware that they form a part of one.

In traditional cultures, or some rural settings, there is a much better chance of seeing mutual give-and-take behaviors. In such environmental surroundings, no one feels that they must give something back to those around them because communal, give-and-take relational activity is what that community's members have been involved in all their lives. Nowadays, however, we have become more and more distanced from those around us and, therefore, feel the need to outwardly demonstrate our gratitude to the society/environment we live in.

I'm hoping that at this point you know why this is the case. Understanding how The Structure that guides us works, no matter what level of developmental sophistication any given social community may have, it is not surprising that there be an underlying sense that members of a community feel indebted to those who form that community. Many community members often feel that they literally owe their lives to everything and everyone around them. This should make perfect sense as, indeed, from a structural perspective, they do.

The vital nature of recognition

As you now know, we care deeply how we think others judge, evaluate, and ultimately value us. We care about such things because others form the very essence of our structurally driven lives. We structurally owe our lives to those around us. Therefore, every piece of positive or negative feedback we receive from our relational surroundings is like either one more breath of fresh air or one more slat nailed to our relational coffin. Whatever or whoever it may be that allows us to value ourselves— be it our makeup kit, toolbox, new car or home, our parents, friends, neighbors, or loved ones, a local bank teller or magazine stand owner—they all contribute to our psychological well-being. If we think that we're judged positively (affirmed), we will feel balanced and free to move about as we must. If, on the other hand, we sense rejection or disapproval (contradiction), we may feel at odds with our environment and, therefore, out of psychological sorts.

Life's relational cold shoulder

There is yet a third relational circumstance of life some of us can be, occasionally, confronted with but whose cause is usually more difficult to pinpoint. We may feel, for example, that our environment is giving us a relational cold shoulder. When this occurs, we perceive only scanty amounts of relational echo from others, a situation that can make us feel ill at ease and suspicious that we may have done something to provoke such a lack of relational support.

All in all, recognition from others forms the very basis of how we get through life. Actually, it's the only way we are able to confirm the most basic of The Structure's imperatives, *relational activity*, coupled with awareness of that activity. Each and every relational recognition we receive—a neighbor's wave, a simple hello, a thumbs up from our employer, or any little bit of positive public attention— enables us to feed our fundamental need to perceive relationally reassuring confirmation from those around us.

Thinking that we've been affirmed by our environment provides feelings of well-being.

Common or shared
relational
experiences unite.

CHAPTER 10

The Relationships That Unite Us

Most of us begin our days in very similar ways: by opening our eyes and looking at our immediate surroundings. Even though we don't realize it yet, our conscious and subconscious minds will have, in the next 24 hours, vastly different experiences than everyone else will. Even if someone else is standing right next to us and experiencing the same objects that we are, what we are each seeing, hearing, tasting, feeling, and smelling will be significantly different from anyone else, even if we spent the entire day exposed to identical circumstances. Given that each one of our genetic backgrounds and the unique physical spaces we occupy may be virtually the same, we will still perceive the world around us, and react to that world, differently than anyone else.

Our similarities and our differences

Despite the often vastly different ways we may react to the same relational experience, the very fact that we are experiencing a common stimulus unites us. After all, we're witnessing the exact same objects and events as everyone else, only from a different perspective and in different ways.

For example, in our story about Heather and Bridget (see "Out of their element" on page 49), each of our adventurous protagonists had very different genetic backgrounds and were brought up in very different relational environments. Yet, they were perfectly able to find common ground through the

experiences they both shared. It didn't matter that the experiences they were having touched each of the two girls in vastly different ways. It was the sharing itself of those experiences that bound them together relationally.

Heather had been subjected to a home life and a set of absentee parents that provoked in her feelings of loneliness and isolation. Her relationship with Bridget, to the contrary, made her feel in touch and supported. It's true that Bridget loved the desert heat, but Heather had second thoughts about it. The tarantula they found made Bridget uncomfortable, unlike Heather, who was delighted to have found it. Once again, affirmation and contradiction played their individual roles, changing who those two young women were becoming as they confronted the same exact relational circumstances and experiences. So what might we say is the psychological moral to their story? ***Common or shared relational experiences unite.***

For example, in the mathematical equation referred to as the transitive property of equality, if A is equal to B, and B is equal to

> **When a common experience is shared by one or more people, those involved become relationally united according to the pain or pleasure they have mutually partaken in.**

C, then C will be equal to A. In Bridget and Heather's case, one could say that Bridget shared a series of common or equal goals with Heather; a relational event that bound them closer to each other. A lack of experience with these kinds of relational equations would equal psychological troubles for just about all of us.

Trapped and alone

As Sam stood with his face to the sky, rain pelted him without mercy, and he began to shake uncontrollably. The man was becoming increasingly aware of just how helpless his situation was, stranded at the bottom of a condemned well that he couldn't, for the life of him, climb out of. He had already been there for more than two days and two nights and was becoming more and more convinced that nobody had noticed he was even missing. "How would anyone know or care where I am? I didn't say anything to anybody before I left. I never do." Belting out repeated cries for help and sporadic

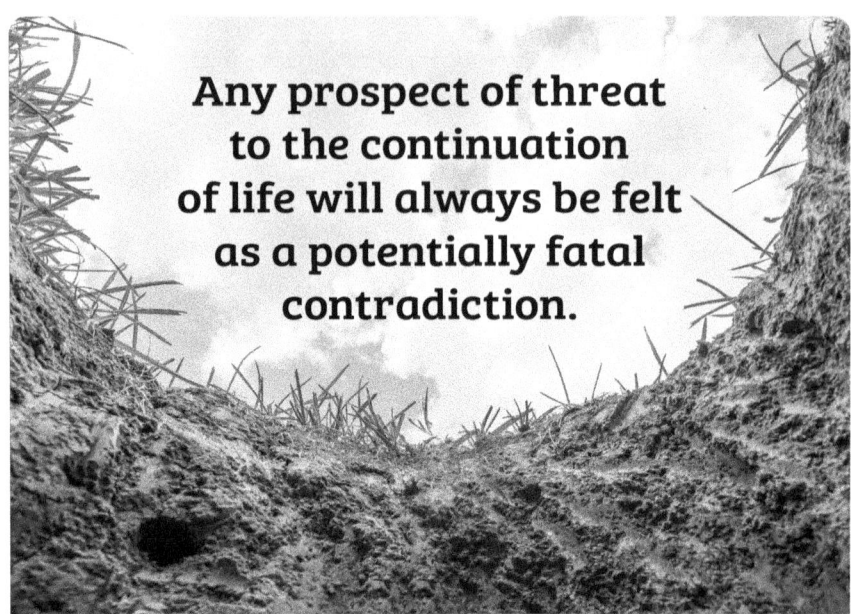

Any prospect of threat to the continuation of life will always be felt as a potentially fatal contradiction.

screams, the hours passed, but with no response, his anxious panic turning into somber dread as he realized the stark reality his future held.

Sam's world had suddenly been reduced to a four-by-eleven-foot darkened pit that, little by little, was filling with water. There was no horizon to anchor him, no response from beyond, not even an echo from his own voice. Sam's life was coming to an end and every emotion in his body was responding to that reality.

When our futures fade

In our story, Sam is not only trapped, but his relational environment has been reduced to just a few square feet, with zero positive confirmations. As a result, Sam is subjected to waves of anxious dread. The continuation of his existence is in serious check, and when one loses their sense of future (i.e., the structured imperative of continuation), they lose their sense of self and, eventually, of life itself.

A bleak future or any prospect of threat to the continuation of life will always be felt as a potentially fatal contradiction. Contradictions of this kind can—and often do—have equally serious psychological consequences that create significant emotional and physical behaviors. Sam's cries for help going unanswered (the absence of relational confirmation) turn his life into a nightmare. He is being profoundly threatened (no viable future, no continuation), and he is on the verge of giving up.

As we've witnessed several times now in other vignettes, the condition or status of our psyches is determined by the positive and/or negative confirmations we receive from the relationships we engage in. When our lives meet our structural needs, we're able to move forward in positive ways. But when our needs and goals are contradicted, certain specific emotions will be triggered, and very specific behaviors will follow.

Our goal-oriented lives

All human behavior involves some form of future-oriented, goal-seeking activity. Some goals can appear, to the untrained eye, as insignificant, like when we absentmindedly scratch an itchy patch of skin, or sigh when feeling anxious. Others are more obvious, like when we start a family, or change our environment and move to another town or city. No matter what the pursuit of a goal may be—regardless of its scale—all goals relate to our *futures*, focus on *who we are*, and point to *who we are continuously becoming.*

All human behavior involves some form of future-oriented, goal-seeking activity. (We are our goals and needs.)

Back to the beginning

Keep in mind that the only difference between the above-mentioned individuals and the life you are leading is those individuals' radically different genetic backgrounds and the vastly different environments they have been subjected to.

So, again, why did that school shooter do what they did? Or why did that music sensation become, all of a sudden, political? They did so for the exact same reasons that we all behave the way we do. They had no choice! Each was simply obeying the norms or imperatives of The Structure that guides the behavior of all living things; a Structure that is anonymous and equal for all; a Structure that prompts each one of our specific and individual genetic backgrounds to continually interact relationally with the world around us. Even though their behavior may be judged in a formal courtroom or in a court of public opinion, all emerging judgments coming from our environment will not be anchored to any scientific principle other than the moral laws of that environment where that judgment takes place.

Digital disconnect

Tommy's new gaming system was a step up from the older one he had before, and he couldn't wait to try it out on the multiplayer game *Sunset City* that was topping the online gaming charts in the virtual reality scene. He put on his VR headset and started to assemble his avatar. He knew he had to come out, guns blazing, because of the big deal he always made to his standard team of players. "Let me play, guys! I *know* I'll totally kick ass!"

"Behind you!" The action started fast, and Alex alerted Tommy that he was about to get taken out by one of the vampires. The warning allowed him to jump out of the way just in time. "Thanks Alex. Let's get those suckers!" Things got intense in a fraction of a second. But Tommy was earning some serious cred in the metaverse, and his crew was definitely gaining the upper hand. As the battle continued, he felt in the zone, closing in on the winning target. But, just as he was about to stake the head vampire right through the heart, Tommy's internet went down, and his player froze, leaving all his vampire-hunting buddies to fend for themselves. The vampires attacked, and he wasn't defending himself. He couldn't. He'd just disappeared from the world of internet gaming!

"Hey Tommy, where did you go?" Alex broadcast over his headset. But there was no response. Tommy was cut off from the action, and all of a sudden it was as if he didn't exist at all. In just seconds he felt the pain that frustration can create, and as a response, threw his controller across the room, shattering it into a thousand pieces.

Even when it's just a game

Tommy's goal was to dominate at *Sunset City*, so he confidently declared his gaming acumen to his buddies (his environment). Unfortunately, in doing so, he opened himself up to being more heavily judged for his performance than any normal player would have been. If he won, however, he wouldn't only get points for control over the contradictions the game world would challenge him with, but also for his level of self-confidence. A real double boost, and this young fellow needed all the double boosts he could get.

Tommy was genetically gifted at playing video games. Even when a game was brand new, he had the innate knack to know how to dominate it. As a result, he expected applause and admiration from his gaming buddies. It had always been that way. He was a natural, a genetically gifted vampire slayer. In Tommy's case, one of his most important sources of relational environmental confirmation was directly linked to his gaming, so that's the vehicle he'd use to get as much affirmation as he could from those who were relationally vital to him.

When Tommy's internet connection betrayed him, it was as if someone had pulled the plug from his soul. He was blocked from demonstrating who he was and could be, leaving him in VR limbo. There would be no exceptional relational activity, no reward for his talents. Tommy's disconnection severed access to the positive environmental confirmation he so desperately needed. As a result, he felt waves of severe disappointment come over him, as well as frustration, anger, and regret. And because he was so invested in this one specific relational activity, the need for neutralization begged him to do *something—anything!* So he demonstrated his rejection of what had failed him...just ask his controller.

Exposure: the effects of effort

The level of confirmation we receive from our relational environments is often impacted by the amount of effort and, therefore, potential exposure we put into trying to reach our objectives. If, after having made an effort to reach a certain goal, we're successful in reaching that goal, we might get a nice pat on the back, a thumbs up, or smiles from all around. If we fail, however, we open ourselves to all manner of negative feedback and subsequent emotional unrest.

On the contrary, if we reach a goal ostensibly making little or no effort at all, we score extra points. Reaching a goal as effortlessly as possible demonstrates to everyone (especially ourselves) that the level of relational control we wield over contradiction merits a lot more than just smiley faces or a gold star.

> The level of confirmation we receive
> for our success is often impacted
> by the amount of effort one has used
> to reach the intention of their actions.
>
> Effortless accomplishments
> demonstrate a high level of control.
>
> Where there is more effort exerted
> in reaching a specific goal, more
> demonstrable involvement in
> reaching that goal will be evident.

Defensive shields, foreshadowing, preempting

As life moves along, we quickly learn ways of defending ourselves from the emotional pain life's contradictions regularly bring to our door. By foreshadowing possible future failures, we can partially defend ourselves from some of contradiction's negative impact.

Many of us learn on the fly how to foreshadow or **preempt** potential contradictions by declaring our disconnection from the skills needed to reach specific goals, a tactic whose intention is to separate us from a possible future contradiction. For example, someone might say, "Sure I'll dance with you, just know that I've got two left feet." "I'll try to sketch it out here, but I'm no Dalí." "I'll gladly make lunch, but I'm no star chef."

Tommy, in contrast, did just the opposite. By bragging about his gaming skills, he doubled down on any possible damaging contradictions he might receive from his environment, setting himself up for a far more intense downside then would have appeared had he simply kept quiet about his intentions.

Freebies vs. earned affirmations

Have you ever noticed how those who pre-announce their intention to reach a specific goal often fail to do so? "I'm going on a diet." "I've signed up to do my master's." "Next Saturday I'll build that shed." "I'll be at Paco's Gym every morning all month." "I just smoked my last cigarette."

And yet, those who keep their goals a secret invariably succeed in reaching them. It's all about waiting patiently to receive the relational affirmations you hope will accompany your efforts to reach a specific goal. Those who receive the applause they're looking for before earning it have a much higher rate of failure then those who don't. This reveals a little-known secret: If you're dead set on reaching a specific objective, keep your plans to yourself, and let the possibility of future affirmation fuel the self-discipline you're going to need to successfully get to where you want to go.

The gal is no Picasso

After Desiree's visit to the Museu Picasso in Barcelona, she felt inspired to try her hand at painting. What she saw profoundly captivated her imagination, making her eager to try her hand at doing some of her own creative work. She already knew she couldn't draw to save her life, but so much of what she had just seen was colorful and geometric—there seemed to be no rules! She'd just experiment and see what happened. How hard could it be?

Weeks passed as she put her whole heart into the endeavor, convinced early on that she would be wowing the world in no time! Soon, however, she began feeling a bit foolish for having thought there was nothing to the precious works of art that so inspired her. Everything she'd created looked like the work of a five-year-old, exhibiting no sophistication or depth. Just chunky paint that wouldn't dry. All the daydreams she'd had about the cheers her art would bring now seemed silly or downright inane, not to mention she was too embarrassed to show her work to anyone anyway.

Inspiration: Is it enough?

Goals can be either 1) genetically motivated, 2) inspired by the behavior of others, or 3) both. In Desiree's case, her desire to paint came from a wish to emulate something she (and so many others) admired. It was her dream to be the focal point of such admiration from those around her. As it turned out,

Any talent you may have is generally derived from your genetic background.

however, this young lady had little talent for art. Talents, like the ability to dance, sing, paint, compose, write, play sports, act, speak other languages, play musical instruments, and so on are invariably genetically born. Talent cannot be taught. It can, however, be awakened, massaged, molded, and built on.

Loving the process!

Often times, our goals become goals simply because we are searching to fulfill The Structure's confirmation imperative, but not because we've been prompted to do so by who we are genetically. Other times, however, who we are genetically prompts us to carry out a specific activity with no other goal in mind than to engage ourselves in the activity itself. Any admiration

Anything you feel compelled to do without the need for compensation or affirmation can help demonstrate where your talents lie.

(positive confirmation) that might gratuitously go along with any successes we might have is experienced as only secondary, not primary in our list of the confirmations we seek.

In the world of filmmaking, for example, you might hear an editor or production designer say, "I just love the process!" or the construction worker quip, "What I like is to build stuff." For people like that, the process itself already provides ample amounts of confirmation, while applause from the environment is but a relational add-on, prize, or perk, but little more.

The genetic self and environmental self in action

We know that each one of our genetic and relational environmental selves is unique. By observing the way life's events affect each one of us, we can gain a better understanding of how the combination of these two entities react to the different situations we experience. For example, how would you react to encountering a tarantula in the desert, dispute territorial rights with a neighbor, or deal with parents who are consistently on a different wavelength? These are all occurrences that can unveil important secrets about one's psychological inner workings. And while it's always been suspected that this was true, now we know why.

Each relational experience we have produces some level or degree of emotional consequence, no matter how apparently insignificant that experience may seem. Much of our lives are filled with mundane background relationships, relationships whose psychological content impacts our mental well-being, but only in subtle ways. Indeed, even the slightest stimulus coming from beyond can affect our behavior without us realizing it. We might associate a song we hear on our car radio with the death of a friend, and suddenly find tears in our eyes. A scent in the air we don't consciously notice might make us feel closer to the person we're with, provoking us to tighten our hand on theirs, or the rustling of trees on an afternoon walk might take us back to our youth, making us sigh and slow our gait.

Can rose-colored glasses change The Structure?

The status of our psychological well-being is not caused by how certain stimuli are processed by The Structure, but rather by the nature of the stimuli themselves. If, for example, someone's central nervous system is affected by physical damage, a shift in the way the brain must carry out its functions may take place, and yet The Structure will continue its normal functions no matter what the structural conditions may be. The only difference will be that the information that passes through its portals will be modified according to how those portals have themselves been affected.

In those cases in which there have been important shifts in our nervous system's status, one might not only suffer from neurological abnormalities but may experience modified versions of the positive and negative confirmations they receive. What before might have constituted a set of manageable contradictions might now, post-trauma, be felt more intensely or, to the contrary, go entirely unnoticed.

Does The Structure hold up at a sub-atomic level?

As we are slowly but surely learning, the quantum world is a world of the impossible where, supposedly, objects can pop in and out of existence from nothing, or a single entity can be in two places at the same time. It's where the laws of Newtonian physics are said to break down, and earthly logic is no longer functional. Could this mean that under such conditions The Structure might break down as well?

If we keep in mind that the quantum world is still an existing world, my speculation would be that no matter what, our quantum existence remains bound by the laws of existence itself. In other words, if we are to come to any firm conclusions about animal behavior at a sub-atomic level, we must not forget that the three imperatives of existence outlined in this book should remain valid. There are no limits to the powerful influence these imperatives wield over all existing things, no matter at what level of existence they may be operating.

Everything experienced by your five senses can lead to associations, and forms a vital part of who you are.

Out of nowhere!

How many times have you surprised yourself by suddenly remembering a place, person, or event from your past that seemed to have absolutely no relationship whatsoever with what you were doing when that memory came to you? For example, you might be having lunch at Barny's Café when you suddenly remember a curve in a road you hadn't driven by in 40 years, or you're walking down the street and a meal you had once in a foreign country comes to mind. A wisp of fresh air, a waft of fabric softener, the texture of a food you're eating, or even a particular position you find yourself sitting in may inspire any number of associative relationships to take place and enter your conscious mind.

What do such incidents have to do with how we are structured? As we have already seen, all relationships are structurally vital to us, despite their position of consciousness. Consequentially, you shouldn't be surprised if suddenly, for no apparent reason, you feel anxious, uneasy, nervous, downtrodden, or elated. Remember, everything you've ever seen, smelled, touched, heard, or tasted forms a vital part of who you are, and only just one unexpected association away from influencing your general conduct.

The way each one of us reacts in relationship to certain stimuli speaks volumes about ourselves (the union between our genetic and environmental selves). The Structure that guides each of us never changes. This simple fact not only narrows down the causes of certain behaviors, but points—with surprising accuracy—to their origin.

In the next chapter, we will continue to explore how seemingly insignificant events can influence the way we conduct our lives, and how such events impact us psychologically.

The Structure that guides us never changes.

The Structure's cause-and-effect dynamics are predictable and point to the origins of our behavior.

All relationships
are structurally
vital to us, despite
their level of
consciousness.

CHAPTER 11

Our Relationally Relevant World

Every relationship we experience causes some sort of behavioral effect at some psychological level. Many of the relationships we engage in can be as subtle as the twitch of an eye or chill felt racing down our back. Indeed, the slightest objective nuance can force us to stop and focus on our surroundings and on our selves. It may seem to us as if we sometimes space out, place our minds on hold, and leave consciousness to the side, but is that what actually happens? Is it possible to turn our consciousness on and off at will?

Consciousness perhaps, but awareness, never! Awareness is that relational sensory bridge over which all relationships, both conscious and subconscious, must travel. Thankfully, The Structure is little concerned about how, or at what level or intensity, relationships take place, just as long as they do!

The daily commute

Fredrick drove the same way to work every day. He'd head east on the only highway between his home and the tech company he worked for. Along the way there wasn't a whole lot to look at. There was that abandoned transistor factory on Henry's Hill as he got on N-5, then that clump of pine trees that lined the westbound side of N-46, followed by Jimmy's Tavern, Austin Beard's Tractor Sales Center, and later the high school. But

Relational relevance is present in all relationally driven psychological events.

Background confirmation takes place any time a relational event occurs.

Fred never paid much attention to any of those things, Instead, he'd usually spend his travel time listening to audiobooks, talk radio, or the learn-French-in-10-days tape his kids gave him for his birthday the year before.

Background confirmation

Like Fred, we've all had the experience of routinely going from one place to another, seemingly paying little attention to much of anything, especially our surroundings. (Or so it would seem.) We passively gaze at things that occupy our visual sphere as we move along, but that's usually because we have nothing better to do. And yet, although we don't think that we notice each passing tree or pedestrian that we whiz by, everything we relate to instantly turns into a part of who we are. This, because although we may not be *conscious* of what we're witnessing, we are, nevertheless, totally *aware* of it. In other words, the psychological impact of all things we relate to may seem of minuscule importance and, nevertheless, whatever we relate to will always be, in some way and to some degree, psychologically relevant.

Back to Fred

Today, Fred was off and running as usual, but this time, as his drive progressed and he turned to get on the N-5, something didn't feel right. All of a sudden, Fred felt confused. Had he gotten on the wrong ramp? He pulled over and stopped. His eyes scanned the horizon. "Where am I?" He continued scanning. His eyes suddenly stopped on a large patch of empty ground. The old transistor factory was gone. It had been torn down over the weekend to make room for new construction.

Relational relevance

As ostensibly meaningless as an old transistor factory might be to the rest of us, to Fred it had inadvertently formed a part of who he was, and now it was gone. Did a tiny part of Fred disappear with it? Of course it did. It had to. It was part of Fred himself! Now it will be its absence that will make up a part of who Fred is.

Did Fred's experience mean that everything that disappears from our environmental backdrop inexorably affects us emotionally? No, of course not! The impact of the relationships we engage in rely entirely on their *relational relevance*. And yet, everything we relate to, especially those objects we relate to repeatedly, will, no matter what, form some part—at some level—of who we are.

Remember how many times you realized that a machine was running in the background, but only when it was turned off? Only then did you realize it had been on in the first place. Indeed, all relational environmental shifts—even those that are subtle—affect us at one level or another. Our lives are filled with experiences, events, and happenings that are, as trivial as they may seem, still relationally relevant.

What is it, then, that's required for a relational experience to be more or less relevant? It all depends on the psychological impact that a relational experience may or may not have on each individual self. That's why you'll often find psychologists and psychotherapists meddling about in their patient's past and discussing what might seem, to the untrained eye, insignificant. They sense that there may be some sort of cause-and-effect relationship in their past that's been negatively affecting the patient's psychological equilibrium, and both therapist and patient want to know what that is.

Our selves, always in flux

We are constantly reinventing ourselves. You, for example, are a different person right now than you were when you began reading this sentence. And although I'd like to think it's because I'm

No living thing can remain divorced from relational activity.

an exceptionally clever writer, I'm pretty sure that's not why you just went through the psychological changes you did. So where did those changes come from? They simply came from the relational activity that took place between the time you started reading the sentence, and the time you stopped. Whatever took place relationally to you during that time affected the person you were continuously becoming. For example, the words you read and what they meant to you, the sounds and scents you unconsciously perceived while you were reading the sentence, someone who in the meantime passed by, and so on all formed a part of your relational day and your relational life. Every minute that you voluntarily or involuntarily relate to your environment and its events, you evolve a little bit more, constantly becoming a new you.

Human behavior—what is it?

From the beginning, I've been using the terms behavior, action, or conduct to refer to the central topic of this book. But what exactly is human behavior? ***Human behavior is any action or reaction that manifests itself within the confines of the human body.*** Any emotion, any feeling, activity, or perception that we experience: a dance we once danced or are dancing right now, a tear we once shed, a dream we're having, and absolutely anything and everything else that we've ever experienced. Our general behavior is what prompts our feelings, thoughts, and actions. Indeed such feelings, thoughts, and actions are behaviors in and of themselves. A loud sound we hear, a shallow sigh, a feeling of happiness, a passing concern, a loving kiss, a casual grimace, or shout for help should all be considered a part of the behavior we humans are so famous for.

No matter how our behavior may manifest itself, it is the direct result of The Structure in action. Without the large and small relational events, we commonly experience every minute of our lives, not only would our mental sanity be seriously challenged, but so would be our very lives.

Human behavior is any action or reaction that manifests itself within the confines of the human body; it is comprised of our thoughts, emotions, feelings, actions, and perceptions.

Our daily lives contain many frequent *constructive contradictions*; they reassure our ability to deal with contradiction and reconfirm The Structure's imperative of continuance.

CHAPTER 12

Constructive Contradictions—
Is There Such a Thing?

Contradictions and affirmations (negative and positive relational confirmations) come in all shapes and sizes. Positive confirmations usually create happiness and contentment, whereas contradictions rarely do. But, again, not all contradictions are the same. Some contradictions, you could even say, are *sheep* in a *wolf's* clothing. These should be referred to as **constructive contradictions**. They are characterized by their ability to move us forward and take to heart a specific task instead of letting it mellow, grabbing opportunities when they appear, proving our worth, or trying something we've never tried before.

You could think of such contradictions as provokers that taunt or threaten but are not yet truly contradicting. These potential contradictions we are, most often, able to overcome or, if you wish, neutralize, with apparent ease. They encourage us to open our eyes each morning and take on the day. They are contradictions that look more like inspiring challenges than destructive paradoxes, and actually invite affirmation instead of its contrary.

Constructive contradictions are easily conquerable (neutralized), serving as reinforcers of the control we wield over ourselves. Examples of such contradictions might appear as a dare that is within our grasp to deal with, a threat that can be effortlessly side-stepped, or any goal that can be reached with little chance of failure. These challenges promise not only to keep us relationally active but reassure us (although often subconsciously) that we are able to deal with contradiction and move forward, thereby reconfirming The Structure's imperative of continuance. And yet, initially, there is nothing positive about them. They are real-life threats of conflict, albeit ones we are accustomed to overcoming in an almost routine fashion.

To understand this structural element better, let's spy on Max before he leaves for his job and see how he deals with the large and small constructive contradictions he encounters.

Morning routine

Max's alarm ripped him away from a dream he was having about flying over the cubicles in his office, amazing friends and coworkers with his extraordinary powers of levitation. Now, back in the real world, he moved quickly to turn the alarm off before it woke Charlie, but he was too late. His partner flipped over with a groan, pulled the pillow over her head, and tried to go back to sleep. It was her day off. But now she was awake.

Like every other morning, the very first thing Max will do is deal with his first constructive contradiction of the day and empty his bladder. Overcoming that first test of control required little thought, which was a good thing, because Max was still half asleep. Then, a morning whiff under the arm, and it's time for a shower. All that nice warm soap and water washed away any remaining thoughts he had of crawling back into bed. Next, off with the whiskers that broke the surface the night

Constructive contradictions are usually easily neutralized, and can be viewed as generally beneficial for our progress, helping us stay motivated.

before, followed by a mouthful of toothpaste to rid him of all the slime that formed over his teeth as he slept. On with his button-down shirt and khakis, then down to the kitchen for a quick scan for something to eat. There, he was surprised to find a fresh pot of coffee waiting for him.

Charlie had decided she might as well get moving because she couldn't fall back to sleep anyway. "You hungry?" she asked.

Max smiled. "If you're offering…" After downing some scrambled eggs and a cup of joe, this young man was ready to tackle another day. After all, he, just like so many of us, just got all warmed up by subduing a laundry list of constructive contradictions and doing so in style.

Our daily grind

Max's little story isn't much of a page turner, I know. Daily life tends to be that way. But his mundane morning routine, when viewed through a structural lens, offers a surprising amount of fodder for thought, at least the psychological kind.

Let's begin with that dreaded alarm clock. Many of us start our day having to face this rude, early morning contradiction. Yet, just by pushing a button, we're able to neutralize its annoying ways. Next, it's time to put our feet on the ground, an action that may produce a few moans and groans— behavior that affirms our disassociation with one of life's most common repetitive contradictions. So far so good! Then it's a question of emptying the bladder. Neutralizing any and all feelings of discomfort delivers us quick shots of relief and micro-feelings of triumph! Then, it's off to take a shower, and some teeth brushing—another successful neutralization. Now, instead of smelling like a dead tiger Max smells like a fresh meadow, and who doesn't like that fresh meadow scent? Next, it's time to dress. Today's modern environments insist we do this. People don't run around naked like they used to back when living in caves was all the rage. So Max puts on something that will keep his relational environment from the outrage they might display were he to arrive at work in his birthday suit. Good job! Then, it's time to deal with an empty stomach (contradiction), so Max eats some breakfast (neutralization). At this point the man's day is decidedly on the right track.

Like so many of the rest of us, Max was able to successfully neutralize each contradicting task he was confronted with, and do so with little or no negative backlash. Once again, someone

The gratification that neutralized contradictions often afford inspires us to create minor contradictions for ourselves so that we can receive the benefits that easy victories can bring.

got their day underway with flying colors! To the contrary, had Max been obliged to deal with contradictions that were harder to neutralize—his day may have gone quite differently. (You can make up that story by yourself. Just as a suggestion, you might start with an alarm clock that someone forgot to set the night before...)

Testing the waters

At this point, if you haven't begun to do so already, you might like to give The Structure a little test drive for yourself and pay particular attention to how you and others behave in structural terms. Pick a day or time, and count the number of affirming or contradicting confirmations you, or someone near you, encounter, and how any ensuing conduct reflects the power behind the behavioral imperatives you've been learning about.

Just remember that everything we feel, think, and do...that's everything with a capital E, is set in motion by those three logically supported structural mandates (imperatives), imperatives that never stop flexing their muscles: relational activity, confirmation, and continuance.

The playful face of contradiction (really!)

For another example of what could be called our binary nature (affirmation/contradiction, subject/object, etc.), take note how we sometimes voluntarily create our own constructive contradictions just to feel the positive results that certain controlled neutralizations can bring. This kind of conduct not only serves to fortify our self-image as accomplished contradiction crushers, but to reduce any self-doubt we might have about our ability to *continue* moving forward in life (a structural imperative).

For example, by eating salted peanuts we'll have an excuse to pour ourselves another cold drink and neutralize our thirst. We might sit out in the hot sun despite the discomfort it provokes just so we can jump into a pool full of cool water and feel the control we wield over our contradictory world. Or we'll eat something sweet so as to justify smoking another cigarette, throw a ball in the air to see how many times we can catch it, tease our dog with a treat only to finally give it to him, or subject ourselves to doing a challenging puzzle.

Everything we think, feel, and do is the result of the relational activity we engage in.

All behaviors
have structural
causes.

CHAPTER 13

Remember Where Your Power Lies

Look around! So far we've had a cursory gaze at The Structure that guides who we are and how we behave. We've seen that it determines how we feel, think, and ultimately conduct our lives. We know that it is relational, continuing, in need of confirmation, and rigorously logical.

Speaking of logic, it's important to keep in mind that this often-used term is no wispy, imaginary, or made-up concept. Logic was discovered, not created, and has formed the basis of behavior—human or otherwise—since the beginning of time! As mentioned before, this doesn't mean that there aren't behaviors, actions, or events that appear to be totally illogical. There are plenty of those. (A discussion for another time!) And yet, the root causes of such seemingly illogical events are, once closely observed, as logical as simple addition.

Just take your own self as an example. Often, your behavior may make little sense. Only now you know that no matter what brand of behavior you may display, it will have a structural and, therefore, logical explanation. For example, if we ever find ourselves scratching our heads wondering where a certain kind of conduct came from, we can always find our way back to solid ground by returning to The Structure's three imperatives and observing how they must have played a role in what we've observed.

To sum things up

Ever since humans first began to interest themselves in the way they conduct their lives, any number of ad hoc philosophical and psychological theories have emerged, many of which have been ingeniously conceived. Experts of human conduct have consistently done their best to explain what it is that inspires us to search for splendor and harmony, but also seek ways of expressing our discord, anger, and nonconformity. Why we care as much as we do about what we *think* others think of us. Why certain events please some, but intensely annoy others, and what it is that drives us to love a fellow human one minute but the next strive to destroy them. Ever since Freud there have been those who have suggested we live by some pleasure principle. Clearly they were onto something. Now at least we know what that something was.

So, is our behavior our fault or not?

Now that we know why it is that we think, feel, and behave the way we do, can any of us honestly say that we are responsible for our own actions? Is the way we live our lives simply the result of

> **Human behavior is the result of the following structurally mandated imperatives: *relationability, continuance*, and *confirmation*.**

us exercising our free will, or is there more to our behavior than meets the eye? Once again, I hope you already suspect what the answers to these questions are.

As we have learned, all living things live their lives according to the genetic and environmental cards they've been dealt and are played out under the strict guise of an all-powerful Structure. There are definitely rules to life, and they are far stricter than anyone ever imagined.

For example, it might seem, from a distance, that Matilda Dean, the meanest person on the planet, chose to be the grumpy old lady that she is, personally relishing the harm she does to others with her annoying demeanor, love of hate, incessant insults, and bad personal hygiene. And yet, now that you know that Matilda arrived at life's doorstep exactly like we all do (involuntary loaded down with a plethora of quasi-immutable genetic material), perhaps you'll have a little more understanding and compassion for Matilda. She's just trying to keep her head above water, do her thing, and continue being true to who she is!

Since the beginning of time, logic has determined the way our lives are structured.

Even when our behavior may seem anything but, it is our structurally logical response to life's circumstances.

Rights and wrongs, good things and bad are the byproduct of environmental circumstance and the way those who participate in that environment decide to judge others. As we have already observed, an environment's moral statutes can flip to their perfect opposite in the shake of a lamb's tail. Remember, there are societies, nations, environments, and religions on this planet where one action is condemned yet in another, the exact same action is not only approved of but held in high esteem.

If it's not your fault—is it anybody's?

If the way we behave is not really our fault, then whose fault is it? To best answer that question, keep in mind that it is not a question of who is responsible for how we live our lives, but rather what. Indeed, it is an impersonal, autonomous, logical Structure that is the ultimate responsible entity that drives our thoughts, feelings, and behaviors. In view of this, and being the loyal souls that we are to The Structure, we now should be able to recognize, respect, and deal rationally with ourselves and those around us.

Live and let live, as they say...at least up to a point.

Alert!

Am I suggesting that nobody be accountable for their actions? Yes, that is exactly what I am suggesting—at least not from a structural perspective. Keep in mind that accountably is an environmental concern, not a structural one. The Structure that guides us doesn't pick sides or play favorites. It has no relevance whatsoever when it comes to society's fluent moral norms or requirements. Nevertheless, given that we are our environment, accountability is real, necessary, and crucial to the way we live our lives. Even though the perception of good and evil can be no more solid state than might be the whim of a tyrant or the latest trend on social media, it still forms an essential part of who we are and are constantly becoming.

> **The Structure is universal, and is the primary reason for our behavior.**
>
> **Moral statutes are not universal; they are derived from the norms of one's relational environment and can change as one's environment changes.**

In conclusion...

You get to choose. You can either live your life in tight coexistence with your environment, its ever-changing moral standards, and apparently ever-changing arbitrary ways, or you can remember what you read here and use the knowledge you've acquired to pry open life's secrets and let their root mysteries confuse you no more. Just remember, understanding why you (and everyone else) think, feel, and behave the way you do can help immensely to polish up your level of tolerance for the workings of the world around you, and those who occupy it. This, very much including yourself.

Understanding and forgiveness

As your knowledge of how we're psycho-existentially structured continues to grow, forgiving those around you for any contradicting behavior they may display should become much easier. To forgive truly is divine.

> **What's deemed acceptable or not has nothing to do with The Structure and everything to do with the environment we live in.**

For best results, when confused or in doubt about someone's behavior, just remember this:

> **The behavior of all existing things is determined by the behavior of existence itself.**

P.S.

If you would like to dive deeper into the secrets of human behavior, I invite you to explore the contents found online. There, you will find the theory explained in detail, a glossary of the terminology I consistently use, several explanatory videos, many more examples of the theory in action, and a comprehensive description of the scientific mooring that I used to unveil The Structure we live by.

StructuredPsychology.com

Dear Reader,

Thank you for reading *It's It's Not Your Fault.* As you know, it is specifically designed to help all of us not only understand our own behavior but also the behavior of others—after all, they go hand in hand! My sincerest hope is that this message spreads worldwide, allowing us all to feel the relief that comes from understanding why we think, feel, and behave the way we do. Filling out the survey below will help us reach this goal.

Thank you,

Rogers Follansbee, PhD

structuredpsychology.com/book-survey

 Rogers Follansbee, PhD, graduated in 1968 from the Universidad de Navarra (Pamplona, Spain) with a master's degree in philosophy. In 1971, he acquired a master's degree in clinical psychology from the Universidad de Madrid. From 1969 to 1974, during his post-graduate studies at the Universidad de Navarra, he instructed undergraduates in "The History of Psychology" and "Psycho Diagnostics." He also held graduate seminars where his theory was discussed in detail to small groups of undergraduates. In 1974, Dr. Follansbee successfully defended his dissertation, "La Teoría de la Relacionabilidad," and was awarded a summa cum laude qualification.

In 1980, Dr. Follansbee and his family moved to the United States, where he continued to develop *Relationability* (now *Structured Psychology*). He and his wife Carmen now split their time between homes in Southern California and northern Spain.

Understanding
why you (and
everyone else)
think, feel, and
behave the way
you do can
help increase your
tolerance of others.

Understanding the way life is structured gives us the power that all knowledge affords those who have it.

Index

Index

Index

Knowing how
we're structured
is the first step
to psychological
wellness.

www.ingramcontent.com/pod-product-compliance
Lightning Source LLC
Chambersburg PA
CBHW051613120626
46551CB00014B/1771